SPEAR SELLING

The ultimate Account-Based Sales guide for the modern digital sales professional

Jamie Shanks

Praise for Spear Selling

Jamie Shanks shares with you his story, his experience making this a sales book that speaks the truth. You need to make this book the first book you read if you're serious about improving your sales process.

Mark Hunter, Author, High Profit Prospecting

~ ~ ~

Spear Selling offers a structured approach that teaches salespeople how to leverage the adjacencies of their existing customers and/or personal relationships in order to increase their sales velocity. I would highly recommend this for a sales leader!

Victor Antonio, Sellinger Group, Sales Trainer & Motivation Keynote Speaker

~ ~ ~

Having led sales teams of more than one hundred sales professionals, getting account based selling right is critical. In SPEAR Selling, Jamie nails it when he says that account selection is the single most crucial element of any account-based selling program. If you haven't been successful implementing account-based selling, this book is built on the realities of today – that social proximity is more important than geographical proximity!"

Chad Burmeister, CEO at ScaleX.ai & BDR.ai, & Sales Author

~ ~ ~

In prehistoric times a spear was a cutting-edge tool that could feed a tribe. What is old is new again and today, in modern selling, using a spear mentality will feed your forecast in a way no other tool can. Great read!

Trish Bertuzzi, Author of "The Sales Development Playbook," CEO of The Bridge Group, Inc.

~ ~ ~

This book should be called The Definitive Modern Sales Playbook because Jamie holds nothing back. If you want to learn what's working for today's buyer, this is your book.

Steve Richard, Founder @ ExecVision

~ ~ ~

Jamie does it again! SPEAR Selling provides clear ideas and real ways to implement something new for yourself and your organization. I can clearly "hear" Jamie in the writing and it's fun, down to earth, doable, and calls out PEOPLE! At the end of the day, buying and selling happens between two people that mutually agree on a course of action. There are some great pearls of wisdom to be found here that, if implemented, can bring new life to your team and revenue to your company. Thanks, Jamie, for putting this book and ideas out there for all of us.

Dionne Mischler, CEO @ Inside Sales by Design

Table of Contents

Preface

One account changed my business career forever. In my first book, Social Selling Mastery, I told a story about the evolution of my consulting career, which owes much of its success to embracing social selling early enough to help pioneer the category. However, the bulk of my growth over the last six years, as a digital sales advisor and trainer, may not have been possible if it wasn't for one account: Vision Critical, a Canadian customer intelligence software and market research company. It's crazy to think that I can trace the hockey-stick-shaped growth of my consulting career from that single account!

In 2012, when I was experimenting with the power of social selling for my business development efforts, I needed one paying customer to test my newly developed Social Selling Mastery® training curriculum. I was introduced to Vision Critical's SVP of Sales, Mark Bergen, who found my ideas (and my apparent eagerness to build a successful company) appealing enough to test out my training. We agreed on a nominal training fee, but in exchange for being paid very little, I somehow conjured up one of the smartest business ideas I've ever had. In the boardroom with Mark, I said: "I'll make you a deal. I will ensure that each sales professional on your team creates at least one sales qualified lead from my training in 60 days. Assuming you're satisfied with the training result, you will agree to field any referral call I send your way for the next year, even if it's your direct competitor!"

Mark happily agreed, and I could tell that he just wanted me to get this business off the ground. He even accepted having those terms put in writing within our signed Statement of Work.

I'll admit that, at the time, I still didn't have a game plan for what would follow once I'd made the Vision Critical sales team successful. Thankfully the training workshop was a success, and the team created 31 sales qualified leads within 60 days. So now I had a story, but I still had no idea where I should go next with that story! I was a lost consultant and sales professional. Night after night I would agonize over how I could win more business effectively. Time was my enemy. I recognized that I had only 168 hours every week to attract new business and that on the 167th hour, my expenses were due. I needed a process that maximized my ROE (Return-on-Effort). I don't remember exactly how I came up with the idea; as with most sales methodologies, I drew on a sprinkling of ideas mashed together from various experiences. My main memory is of drawing out my plan on a sheet of paper as if I was Dr. Brown from the movie Back to the Future, and I'd just developed The Flux Capacitor. See example:

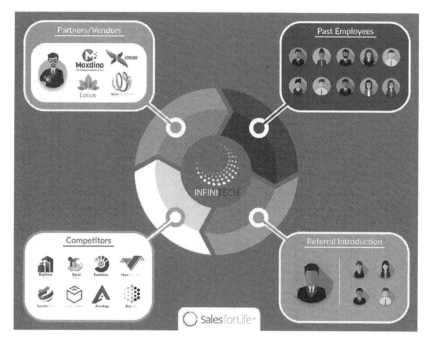

I started by drawing the Vision Critical logo onto the center of a sheet of paper; I then circled it and drew spokes radiating from that circle. I then would look at my drawing and ask myself "who actually cares about my Vision Critical success story?" I would just sit and think about it, and the more I really thought about my story, the more I found my thoughts drifting into the mindset of a customer. It was then that I realized that I was making the same grave mistake many sales professionals do – telling stories to customers that just don't care about that particular story. They don't care because THAT story isn't relatable to THAT particular PERSON. Eureka! People buy from people, and people like people just like themselves. And people listen to stories that they can actually envision themselves being part of. It was through this customer-centric mindset that I began to draw my first "Sphere of Influence" around a particular customer. I started by drawing a list of people and companies that I felt would be most interested to hear about Vision Critical and/or hear about Mark Bergen's success.

September 2012 was when my fortunes changed. At last I had a sales process that was becoming clearer to me. I could see which people and companies I should logically approach because of my Sphere of Influence drawing. My theory was sound, but my methodology had not yet been tested. Time for an attack plan! On September 11, 2012, I wrote a blog on our Sales for Life website about the Vision Critical success story. That gave me a visual reference that I could guide future buyers to, and some real-life results that made my story more credible. Next, I crafted two email messages – one that focused on both Vision Critical's 31 sales qualified leads in 60 days, and one on Mark Bergen's success as a sales leader creating 31 sales qualified leads in 60 days. Finally, I used LinkedIn to map the accounts that had the highest social proximity to Vision Critical and Mark Bergen. I then began engaging VPs of Sales and Marketing on LinkedIn, using InMails and free group messaging. Here's what happened next:

1. Vision Critical had a competitor in Los Angeles called UsAMP. I had met their VP Sales, Kevin Gaither, at the April 2012 AA-ISP Leadership Summit in Dallas, TX. I emailed him the blog story on September 12, 2012, and won their business on February 27, 2013.
2. Mark Bergen was connected to a sales leader at Paragon Relocation, in the corporate relocation

industry. I met their team on a conference call on October 18, 2012, and won the business on November 19, 2012. The success of their project created a tangent Sphere of Influence success story in the corporate relocation industry, which attracted MSI Mobility on March 4, 2013 and won that business on March 26, 2013.

3. Having read my Vision Critical blog, on December 21, 2012 Ronan Keane, a marketing leader at XO Communications, emailed me to discuss the successes from Vision Critical. On January 25, 2013 XO Communications became a customer. Within weeks of that project, their competitor Tata Communications heard about the Social Selling Mastery® training. On March 13, 2013, Tata Communications became a customer. The success of helping two telecommunications leaders allowed me to create a Sphere of Influence that connected me to MTS Allstream in Canada on May 15, 2013 and won their business on July 18, 2013. This telecommunications Sphere of Influence would go on to pay long-term dividends, as we've worked with dozens of telecommunications companies since.

4. The success of working with Kevin Gaither, a prominent figure at AA-ISP events, afforded me an invitation by Bob Perkins (the AA-ISP CEO) to speak at their upcoming event in Arizona in the spring of 2013. This was my first speaking opportunity ever, and it turned out I was good at public speaking. My appearance on stage enhanced my profile and, combined with my Sphere of Influence story with Kevin Gaither, I was introduced to Jill Rowley who was recently leading the global Social Selling program at Oracle. On June 10, 2013, Oracle became a customer.

Let's put this one-year chain of events together. My simple motion of selecting accounts based on high social proximity leapfrogged my business from a $2,500 engagement with Vision Critical to the largest Social Selling training deployment in the world, with 23,000 Oracle sales professionals by the fall of 2013. The Oracle account paved our path for global training engagements on a scale that I hadn't imagined possible in 2012.

Account-based selling was a process long before digital sales, and will continue to exist long after digital becomes standard operating procedure in sales organizations. Digital is only an accelerant to an effective process, and it's the simplicity of the process that we at Sales for Life have designed that makes this so special. Account-based selling is not about tricks or tools, but about aiming and deploying the right stories at the right people. I hope the principles in this book change the course of your sales pipeline, sales team, business unit, or company, as they did for me.

—Jamie Shanks

Introduction: SPEAR Selling executive summary

> "If you can't describe what you are doing as a process, you don't know what you're doing."
> – W. Edwards Deming

The most important takeaway I'd like you to gain from this book is to develop your account-based sales strategy focused on being **process-centric**, not platform-centric. Platform proficiency is only a mechanism for executing your sales strategy. Platforms are communication vehicles, data organizers, data analyzers – but they are not the strategy itself. Teams that focus too heavily on which tools they need to execute their sales strategy tend to fall short of their desired outcome.

Let's take an analogy. If I were sailing a boat from New York City to Dublin across the Atlantic Ocean, should I spend most of my mental energy on:

a: The process of reading navigational charts, trip markers, distance per day goals and mastering food rationing; or

b: The brand of ropes, sails, and crackers, as tools that we'll bring on the trip?

I'm sure you laughed at how obvious this sounds for a life-or-death voyage across the ocean, but the truth is that most sales and marketing leaders, along with sales professionals, focus on tools, tools, tools. They can't see the glaring misalignments in their account-based programs.

This book is meant to be your strategic roadmap, your primer, your order-of-operations for defining and executing your program. There are five parts to your account-based sales process. My most sincere advice is that you start by taking one step backwards and design your process in advance – that's going to help you leap three steps forward. Having trained and advised 300 global companies at the time of this writing, we've seen that the companies that have the greatest success are those that really focused on designing a customer-centric process at the start, then colored in the details with tools, content and sales plays.

Part 1 – SELECT your accounts with a Social Proximity mindset

We truly do believe that account selection is the single most important element of any account-based selling program. If you spend too much time with the wrong accounts, you adversely affect your ability to reach your business outcomes (typically measured in sales quota attainment). When I say "wrong", I mean that your account selection process is far too heavily weighted on "wallet-share" account selection. Wallet-share account selection means that you select accounts in a specific territory or vertical based on that account's potential spend (Average Contract Value, Total Lifetime Value). While the economics of this account selection process makes sense on a spreadsheet (focus on the big fish first), the reality is that sales cycle velocity and probability of winning are major factors that spreadsheets don't account for. And let's remember that these are typically accounts that your competition (and just about everyone else in adjacent industries serving these accounts, who you compete with for 'mindshare') also wants as customers.

Best-in-class account-based selling teams complement their wallet-share account selection with "social proximity" selection. Social proximity is the relationship connectivity between people and/or companies. The process that you'll use to determine social proximity is what we call the "Sphere of Influence". By having a customer-centric mindset, the Sphere of Influence starts by reverse-engineering your existing customers and advocates (people working inside your customer base that use and love your solution). Thinking outwards from inside your customer base, you begin to map both companies and people that have the highest social proximity to your best success stories. These people or companies might be past employees of your customers, competitors, vendors, partners, fellow alumni of your school, key social connections to your best advocates. High social proximity accounts tend to have shortened sales cycle velocity, coupled with increased probability to winning the account, all due to relationships. This becomes your sustainable Asymmetrical Competitive Advantage, which no competitor can take from you. I'll also show you how to map accounts where you have Asymmetrical Competitive Disadvantages, in which your competition may have the upper-hand based on high social proximity, so you can avoid those landmine-laced accounts.

Part 2 – PLAN your sales plays with storyboards

It's said that 85% of people are visual learners. Take a step back and think about how the modern buyer learns today – videos, infographics, comic book-style content consumption. By thinking like a customer, you begin to visualize the stories that would be most valuable to them. Just like writing a movie script (or indeed the creation of this book), the best design process is with storyboards. Your process will need a multi-story, multi-touch plan for each account. No modern-day customer is pushed off their status quo with one magical message. The value of storyboarding your messages also helps keep you accountable to thinking through various message themes, styles, data-points, and engagement mediums. Flawed account-based sales processes that I've seen will deploy multiple touches to an account, only to recognize later that every touch-point is just a slight variant on their original messaging. It's basically a broken record, and the customer isn't learning anything new after the first engagement.

We recommend that you develop at least five storyboards for your future account engagements. We call these engagements "sales plays", exactly like running a play in football, basketball or hockey. Each sales play is varied in its theme, style, data-points and value to the customer. Here is a quick look at those five sample sales plays:

a. **Sales Play 1: The Sphere of Influence connection** We typically see this sales play as the first engagement with the customer. The purpose of this sales play is to both humanize yourself and demonstrate the high social proximity that you and the customer share. This sales play disarms the customer's apprehension of unsolicited engagement, and helps to push them off their status quo.

b. **Sales Play 2: Stack-ranking the account vs. competition vs. best-in-class** The purpose of this sales play is to bring empirical evidence to the customer that objectively showcases **their** strengths, weaknesses, opportunities or threats. (Gartner's Magic Quadrant is a successful example of this.) Customers tend to live in a bubble, and rarely have a well-developed idea of where they benchmark against their peers.

c. **Sales Play 3: Market intelligence and trends** This sales play is an excellent mechanism for building a "trusted advisor" status with a customer. You bring advanced-level business acumen that predicts/pontificates on market trends, or provides industry secrets that help bond you and the customer. In time, you become their trusted resource center.

d. **Sales Play 4: What does the Emerald City look like?** The purpose of this sales play is to visualize and/or experience what success would look if they became a customer. In the movie *The Wizard of Oz*, how could you reduce Dorothy's apprehension about travelling down the Yellow Brick Road and into the scary forest? Show her what the Land of Oz and the Emerald City look like in advance, right at the beginning. Let her see it into a crystal ball, touch it, visualize walking around it, and then watch her excitement grow as she begins her journey. The talking trees and the flying monkeys won't seem so daunting anymore! Show your customers what success looks like 90, 180, 365 days into the future.

e. **Sales Play 5: Role/function career guidance** The final sales play has a different purpose, which is to recognize that you're trying to win accounts by winning over people. People are at the center of purchasing solutions. Rather than just focusing on account-centric messaging, think through the role/function of the buyer. How can you personally help them? What value could you offer that particular person that will strengthen your personal relationship? The sales professionals that master this sales play create customers for life.

These sales plays will all reside within an Activation Cycle. Your Activation Cycle will be an objective process that each account is qualified and activated within to produce next sales actions, or disqualified due to non-activation. This process uses structured thinking, is time bound, and designed with a pre-defined cadence/sequence. The value in running a defined Activation Cycle is to help you objectively focus on the right accounts that will highly influence your sales objectives, and not allow subjective attachment to any account (brand name logos, for example) to distort your sales process.

Part 3 – ENGAGE your accounts with your prescriptive sales plays

Time management on accounts can either be your asymmetrical competitive advantage or your Achilles heel. Managing time effectively is the pendulum that sales professionals, leaders, teams and sales organizations often neglect to focus enough on. This is why so much of our process-centric mapping is done in advance – with account selection/de-selection, planning and storyboarding all happening before customer engagement. I urge you to exercise one more planning element before customer engagement: think through your account segmentation strategy after you've engaged and activated accounts. What naturally happens during account engagement is that some accounts show buying intent, and some do not. You create a slow descending "death spiral" if you don't plan this in advance, and unproductively spend an equal amount of time and energy on each of your accounts. Sales leaders are typically to blame for this. They have designed a sales process that's based on carpet bombing an equal number of sales touches (talk-time minutes, number of calls or emails per day, etc.) to every account, and then just manage to that process. Best-in-class account-based sales organizations, in contrast, will design an account segmentation process in advance, allowing them to clearly define the expected time and energy that should be spent on specific account categories to maximize ROE (return-on-effort).

Once you have your accounts selected, planned and storyboarded, you can infuse your sales plays into digital sales tools and social platforms. Digital sales tools and social platforms (elements of social selling) allow you to engage more customers, more quickly, and with more richly-storyboarded content. They also help you to segment accounts based on buying intent while allowing you to better map the buying committee. In this book I'll showcase best-in-class tools that we leverage, or our customers leverage, and their specific use cases for you to mirror.

Part 4 – ACTIVATE your engaged accounts with tailored learning paths

As customers begin to demonstrate buying intent and are activated, your account segmentation plan becomes highly valuable. How will you **continue** to push key stakeholders in an account off their status quo and align everyone together on their buying journey? We call this nurturing process "learning paths". The customer is going to learn with or without you, so you'd better design a process and action plan to become their resource during their buying journey. There are three natural paths that key stakeholders (remember you're selling to PEOPLE, not just to accounts) will take:

a. **Learning path 1: the dead zone** This is the path you encounter most often, and no doubt the one you loathe. This is the uncomfortable silence you get from customers that either show zero engagement, or show some engagement but then go dark. What will be your game plan to ignite the flame of interest? How long does your ROE (return-on-effort) continue to make sense, before you consider replacing this account with another?

b. **Learning path 2: the Yellow Brick Road** Yes, I must have watched *The Wizard of Oz* too much as a child! The Yellow Brick Road theory is that some buyers find their problem, or your solution, so outrageously complex that they can't get their heads around it. They are prevented from moving forward or making logical decisions because they can't see through the dense, dark forest. This learning path theme will be centered around making the complex seem very linear, logical, and manageable. You will teach this key stakeholder what to prepare for –

obstacles, pitfalls, challenges, success metrics – and (most importantly) **how** to simply move forward and buy.

c. **Learning path 3: the mental pretzel** There are some frustrating key stakeholders that think your product or service seems so simple. They talk about your solution like they could almost do it themselves tonight in their garage. Customers treat the purchase as trivial without factoring in other variables, and will make snap purchase decisions without thinking through the ramifications. This often leads to later regret about how they approached the purchase. This learning path theme is centered around making the simple seem much more complex, and showing how it integrates with bigger decisions. This helps customers stop taking the easy road with small purchases, instead thinking through a more strategic buy.

Part 5 – RUN OR REPLACE your accounts

Best-in-class account-based sales organizations have very defined Service Level Agreements (SLAs) for each sales professional, based on:

a. The Total Addressable Market (TAM) of a territory, and the percentage of accounts that are expected to be activated within a target market;

b. How many accounts can be effectively managed (both minimums and maximums);

c. How long an account can be held for attempted activation, or confirmed dormant, before being replaced with another account.

We call this Service Level Agreement an Activation Cycle. In this book, we will help you design your Activation Cycle. I will help you define the parameters, and create a prescriptive process with two options:

   a. You run your defined sales plays and learning paths against an account, until your Activation Cycle is complete, or closed-won / closed-lost;

and/or

   b. You replace any non-activated / dormant accounts with new accounts, using high social proximity, and these accounts are placed within an Activation Cycle.

This is a dynamic process. It doesn't have you closing a fiscal year and cleansing your CRM of accounts each year. This is a structured process that's kept accountable by sales leaders during quarterly reviews (often a QBR is used as the lagging indicator and "replace date" for accounts, and weekly one-on-ones as the leading indicator to which accounts might be replaced over the upcoming quarter). You, as sales leader, will use targeted questions in your one-on-ones to help keep your sales professionals focused and accountable:

   1. What accounts have you selected and why?
   2. What is the most logical path of entry into that account?
   3. How is that account going to highly influence your sales objectives over other specific accounts you could be targeting? (Opportunity cost)
   4. What is your engagement and activation strategy, and what specific actions have you taken?

The entire Run or Replace strategy is structured to concretely outline the TAM of every sales territory, and set milestones for increasing market share / penetration in each territory.

How do I use this book?

This book was designed with an order of operations that mirrors the Sales for Life – Digital Sales Mastery® program. I've written the book for both sales leaders (look at coaching sales plays), and sales professionals (executing sales plays), as a step–by–step guide to follow. I highly recommend you start with the following:

1. Put one foot in front of the other
You don't just hoist the sails on a new boat and begin tacking into heavy winds, sailing deeper into the ocean without a destination and navigational map. Using this analogy, you also don't start engaging accounts before you logically think through WHY you're engaging those accounts (selection) and plan what information is most important to those accounts (storyboarding).

This book is the result of working with hundreds of best-in-class sales organizations that have built exceptional account-centric programs. Some of our customers have literally become the global defacto standard by which account-based selling is measured. Build your program using the same order of operations that I've laid out for you here. If you need to pause on a chapter, and take weeks to design storyboards with marketing, do it! The upfront work you put into the planning process will be reflected in both sales results and increased value for your customers.

2. Think process-centric, before you execute platform proficiency
At the time of writing, we have three ongoing training engagements where our customers sales and marketing operations teams had purchased LinkedIn Sales Navigator, employee advocacy tools and/or video platforms, all totaling hundreds of thousands or millions of dollars, only to find these tools all eroding into "shelfware" in their businesses. Now the CFOs of these companies are breathing down the sales and marketing leaders' necks, wondering why adoption and usage of these tools are so abysmal.

Remember: a tool or platform is only the accelerant and mechanism to execute your sales plays. It is NOT the strategy and process in itself. As I've seen countless LinkedIn Sales Navigator purchases turn sour, let's use that tool as an example. LinkedIn is the world's greatest database and an incredible communications medium, but the tool itself doesn't execute your sales play! You, the sales professional that has the license to LinkedIn, executes the sales play. If you were the coach of a sports franchise, you'd work on designing effective plays and keeping the team accountable for executing these plays. If you don't get those plays working to drive your results, then the players on the field can have the shiniest equipment in the league... but you're still going to suck on the scoreboard! There is no way their equipment alone will win football, basketball, or hockey games. Design the plays first, then purchase the shiny tools in the quest to accelerate your sales plays.

PART 1: SELECT your accounts with a Social Proximity mindset

Chapter 1: Defining – motions, learning paths, sales plays, and cadences/sequences

"Definitions are the foundation of reason. You can't reason without them."
Robert M. Pirsig

Before we begin building our account-based sales strategy, let's make sure we have complete alignment of standard terminology. This will help you course-correct the vernacular your team uses internally. All of these terms will be elements within your designed Activation Cycle – Service Level Agreement, which each sales professional will execute on each of their accounts.

Motion
A particular go-to-market sales strategy that a team or organization uses to deliver a solution to its customers. Essentially, an account-centric focus, once put into a process and actioned, is a motion. You may choose to execute an account-based motion for only specific sales professionals, selling specific solutions, and/or targeting specific accounts. Not every sales professional in your organization is, or should be, an account-based sales professional. In fact, I would argue that a hybrid approach of **Open-account** and **Account-based** selling is ideal for most companies. As an example, in our company (Sales for Life) we create new opportunities using five distinct sources:

    a. Inbound marketing
    b. Outbound account-based selling
    c. Channel-driven
    d. Customer referrals

    e. Customer expansion

At the time of writing, our inbound marketing motion is not account-based. We leverage a classic open-account focus based on our ICPs (Ideal Customer Profiles) that meet our firmographic, demographic and buying behavior parameters. All this data is delivered to our sales professionals from HubSpot, our marketing automation software.

Cycle timeline
The number of days, weeks, months or years that one account is expected to be managed by a sales professional, in the pursuit to RUN (activate the account) or REPLACE (non-activation or dormant account). This timeline can be different for specific sales professionals, such as mid-market vs. enterprise accounts. Best-in-class sales organizations use historical data from average sales cycles to design this framework, which helps minimize the possibility of a sales professional "holding on" to an account beyond normal sales cycle timelines.

Learning path
Key stakeholders in your accounts are people. People have biases, priorities and learning challenges. Learning paths are different than the classic marketing "buyer's journey" because you recognize that you're educating people within accounts, not accounts themselves. A classic buyer's journey might be:
1. Awareness
2. Consideration
3. Decision

In my previous book, *Social Selling Mastery*, we simplified that language for sales professionals, focusing on three questions that buyers ask themselves (Why, How, Who). In an account-based motion, I believe we need to focus more intently on a key stakeholder mindset.

The learning path thinks more about the specific questions, hurdles and stumbling blocks that specific people (key stakeholders) may encounter, and identifies where you can easily recognize these inflection points. The core difference between a buyer's journey and a learning path is that a buyer's journey attempts to bundle accounts into likeminded sales stages. As an example, a buyer's journey creates content for a VP Human Resources that has naturally progressed from Awareness to Consideration to Decision. A learning path recognizes that this particular VP Human Resources is stuck on a few key points around our implementation process. She's clearly not understanding what we're talking about – in fact, she seems more confused than when we started our discover call six weeks ago. Instead of pushing "Consideration" marketing materials to this VP Human Resources (which will only frustrate her), a learning path asks: "How can I unbundle her confusion, and place her on a path to make this complexity much more simplified?" The sales professional then prescribes a course of insights (perhaps both educational and experiential) for that key stakeholder to absorb. A learning path is more situational than a buyer's journey developed by marketing. Not all like-minded buyer personas would be interested in a standard "nurture path" that marketers design.

Learning paths are very common in learning and development circles, where student A is prescribed different learning materials than student B, based on their competencies and goals. As a sales professional, or sales leader of an organization, you should be treating your accounts (and the key stakeholders inside these accounts) with a similar teacher-to-student mindset. In our experience, key stakeholders fall within three required learning paths:

1. "I'm happy sticking with the status quo."
2. "I'm completely confused/overwhelmed with complexity/choice/not clearly seeing what the end result will be." (Also known as "can't see the forest through the trees.")
3. "I'm certain someone in my company could do this! This seems simple enough. Why do we need you?"

Sales plays
Engaging the key stakeholders in an account through a series of stories designed to create a singular outcome. A single sales play can be made up of multiple sales actions. In football, a play is drawn up, and the players will run around the field for a few minutes trying to execute that series of actions to create one outcome (a first down). Similarly, a sales play might have a series of touch-points as actions inside the play, such as a short burst of phone calls, email,

social, video, live events, mail, etc., but centered around one topic/theme that can deliver an expected outcome. A complete series of sales plays run to fruition is what make up one Activation Cycle.

Cadence/Sequence

These terms are used interchangeably; neither is right or wrong. I prefer to use cadence as the time between sales plays, and sequence as the order of operations in which you'll execute each sales play – all part of your sales play architecture. What's best practice? How many sales plays, and the time between plays? Going back to our football analogy, imagine a play called "44 Jet Long", which has the quarterback in shotgun, prepared for a deep pass into the end zone. The sequence dictates WHEN this sales play should be used, and the cadence dictates HOW long this play should be run after a big running first down. In the same way, sales organizations will design various cadence/sequences in a series, based on a number of specific sales plays to be deployed over a specific time duration (the Activation Cycle). In examples used in this book, we might choose five sales plays, in a cadence deployment of 30-days and sequences in a specific order-of-operations to tell a linear story, to conclude our Activation Cycle.

Touch-points

The individual action used within a single sales play. The touch-point is the most common measurable that a sales leader can use as a leading indicator to ensure a sales professional is on track to highly influence their sales objectives. As mentioned before, these touches can be digital (LinkedIn, Twitter, WhatsApp, video email), analog (phone, mail), or experiential (live event, coffee meeting).

Chapter 2: How account selection radically alters your business outcomes

"Efficiency is doing things right; effectiveness is doing the right things."

Peter Drucker

I remember my very first week as a rookie sales professional in commercial real estate, in November 2004. I was assigned a group of accounts in Etobicoke, part of Toronto's far west neighborhoods. In the commercial real estate world, a neighborhood within a city is known as a node, and this particular node is exactly where you put a rookie sales professional. At the time, Etobicoke was a place where doctors' offices, small non-profits and family-run businesses would have their offices for long periods of time. This was not a high income-producing node for commercial real estate brokers. My first task was simple: ride the subway into Etobicoke (armed with business cards, a suit, and a shiny smile), walk into each office and introduce myself. "Building walks", as they're called in the industry, were used for two purposes at that time:

a.   To stack-design a building's floor plate on a sheet of paper, so that you could visually map all tenants (software and centralized lease records on all tenants didn't exist then);
b.   To introduce yourself, in order to start developing a relationship with the company.

The data I collected was kept for my records only, at my desk in a pile of other building floor plates. Day after day, I would walk around Etobicoke and map the commercial buildings, one tenant at a time. I was filled with energy, and couldn't wait to start placing calls and booking meetings with the C-level executives that run these tenanted companies. One week later, I had mapped the entire Bloor West subway line for commercial tenants, and was ready to start making calls. What I did next is the classic mistake of sales professionals around the world after mapping their Total Addressable Market (TAM), and beginning their initial account selection process.

    a.   I double-checked each company against records in our CRM. If that company wasn't in the CRM, I would enter a new account.

    b.   I built a call list (on a sheet of paper) of 50 companies I would call first. The design of that list was simple: I would start calling those farthest west on the Bloor subway line (as fewer brokers focused on that area), and work my way east towards downtown Toronto.

    c.   I leveraged the internal "call accountability" document (printed on a sheet of paper). I needed to achieve 12 sales conversations a day, and I would use as many touch-points as it took to achieve that outcome.

That's it – welcome to my account selection process at that time! Can you see any holes in my plan? The end result was simple over the next three months: BURN OUT. My roommate's mom actually sat me down a few months into the job, and said that I would probably drop dead at an early age if I kept working so hard. I was working efficiently, not effectively. In calling every company in Etobicoke in an attempt to achieve results, I was being efficient in what was asked of me (call accountability) but not effective in my outcomes. I specifically remember a time in December 2004 when I didn't see sunlight for three days, because I had woken up so early to get to the office and left so late at night. That's not glamor or pride talking, it's the sad reality of my "work hard, not smart" strategy. Sure, I booked a ton of meetings, and I impressed our CEO with my work ethic, but it still didn't yield the type of results I needed to hit sales quota. What I really didn't understand was that smarter account selection would alter the effectiveness of my efforts, and maximize my ROE (return-on-effort). No matter how well I prepared my call planning, or designed the best sales plays, my account selection process was impeding my progress.

What is "wallet-share" account selection?

Forget my ridiculous commercial real estate story – that's clearly what rookies do. Right? Unfortunately senior sales professionals, sales leaders, and C-level executives also make the mistake of developing "strategic or targeted account lists" based on a concept we call "wallet-share thinking". I have heard this story from customers, probably a hundred times: "Our account executives (AEs) are responsible for selecting their accounts in their territory, and they give that selected list to their sales/business development representative (BDR or SDR). They create a list of accounts they would really like to win this year." Yes, you read that correctly: accounts are selected on… glamorous logos. The process used for "wallet-share" account selection is typically based on attributes such as:

a. The number of employees
b. Market share
c. Topline revenue
d. Appearance on a list in a trade publication, newspaper or magazine

I'm going to set the record straight up front – having a portion of your account selection focused on winning highly strategic accounts, even if based on wallet-share, is still highly strategic. Your company (and perhaps you personally) has a lot to gain from winning an account that can potentially secure you:

a. Super-sized Customer Lifetime Values (LTV)
b. Initial or deeper penetration in a new vertical or geographic territory
c. Publicity
d. Internal excitement that boosts morale because of that account's brand cachet

There are so many reasons a company chooses strategic accounts. Heck, I can personally tell you that we at Sales for Life have targeted and won specific accounts with a negative Customer Acquisition Cost (CAC)-to-Customer Lifetime Value (LTV) ratio, simply because we knew the account posed incredible branding opportunities. But that doesn't mean that your Activation List, or the entire sales organization's account selection strategy, needs to be filled with these types of accounts. As I mentioned before, a common mistake is the misguided focus an account executive provides their lead generation counterparts (marketing, SDR/BDRs, demand generation). The account executives are assigned specific geographic territories or verticals, and they tell their lead generation counterparts to reach out to company X, Y, Z. In nearly every company we've encountered, that account selection criteria was nothing more than wallet-share thinking, based on gut-feel and brand recognition. You have no more strategic advantage in these accounts than your competitor does. You potentially have no more insights or relationships into these accounts than your competitor. The most likely outcome is that you extend all your sales cycles to the maximum velocity expected, hindering cash flow, and adversely affecting sales quota attainment.

What is "social proximity" account selection?
When I was 16, I started a landscaping company in my small town of Manotick, Ontario, Canada. I made pink and yellow flyers that I photocopied at Mac's Milk convenience store, and handed them out door-to-door. Just as I was about to start my first spring lawn cutting season, my mother said to me "Jamie, if you do a great job, two people in the neighborhood will hear about you; if you do a terrible job, eight people in the neighborhood with hear about you". She paused, looked at me intently, and I could see what she was really saying: "The neighbors will tell me, and I'll feel embarrassed... so don't screw up!" Even as a teenager, I was learning about the power of business development through social proximity and successful storytelling.

> "It is six to seven times more expensive to attract a new customer than it is to retain an existing one."
>
> *– ThinkJar*
>
> "4.2x more likely to get a sales appointment if you have a relationship than if you don't."
>
> *– Sales Benchmark Index (SBI)*

Social proximity account selection is about using your Asymmetrical Competitive Advantages (customer successes, relationships and personal experiences) as the centerpiece of developing targeted account lists within a specific territory or vertical. This strategic process thinks outward from a customer-centric core, rather than just using subjective biases (such as thinking about the BIG COMMISSION score). The core purpose of this mindset is to find these asymmetric competitive advantages that you or your sales organization has in account(s), that others (namely, your competitors) just can't compete against. If your brother or sister was working at a big corporation that's a great account for your company, wouldn't you use your high social proximity to give your company an asymmetric competitive advantage over your rivals? Now imagine that these leverage points exist around every happy customer served by your company, and also around the people (advocates) working within those customers. This modelling begins to open up a compound level of opportunities as you create more happy customers in a territory or vertical. Social platforms like LinkedIn can provide you with the insights to understand how these relationships are all interconnected.

Chapter 3: The Sphere of Influence account selection process

> "It's not the strongest of the species that survives, nor the most intelligent, but the one most responsive to change."
>
> Charles Darwin

We at Sales for Life have polished the Sphere of Influence framework since its inception in 2012, as we were looking for the most efficient path to growth. When we launched our initial services, we were stuck in a basic sales quandary – we had very limited time until we ran out of money, and yet we had thousands of potential accounts to target in the Toronto market. Where should we start? In 2010 and 2011, my personal analog sales instincts had me focused in the wrong direction. I picked up copies of both *Inc.* and *Profit* magazines, looking for their lists of the fastest-growing companies. I circled the companies with headquarters in Toronto and I began to call, one by one. Man, did I waste a lot of time! Day in, day out, I would call sales leaders and talk about our various sales consulting services. I didn't get very far. Yes, given time (I mean lots of it) I would probably crack into one of these accounts. And yes, the value of these accounts (both financially and for brand recognition) would have been excellent. But the likelihood is that I would have run out of money before this ever materialized. It wasn't until I designed the Sphere of Influence account selection process that my fortunes changed.

What is Sphere of Influence account selection?
This is the overarching framework that leverages Asymmetrical Competitive Advantages that you and your sales organization have over your competition – relationships with high social proximity! These accounts (and the key stakeholders within these accounts) are easier to influence in their decision-making process because of

their high social proximity to **your** successes, customers and/or advocates. In essence, they can relate to your stories.

Your company's Sphere of Influence may include:
a. The employees who currently work at your customers;
b. The previous employees of your customers;
c. The competitors to your customers;
d. The vendors and partners associated with/supplying your customers.

Your own personal Sphere of Influence may include:
a. Your family;
b. Your friends;
c. Your sports, community and/or religious social network;
d. Your previous school alumni.

Each of these relationships creates varying degrees of asymmetrical competitive advantages for you! These are experiences and relationships that your competitors can't easily replicate.

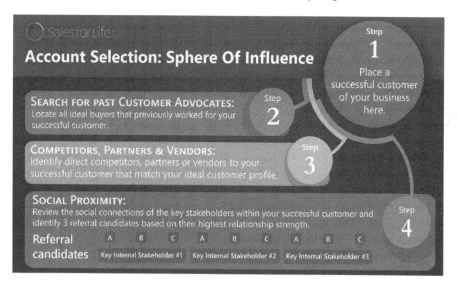

Starting your Sphere of Influence account selection process

If you are a sales professional, I would like you first to clear your mind of any predetermined named or targeted accounts that you've already focused on. For most sales professionals globally, some of your targeted accounts have been assigned to you for various reasons, but a portion/percentage of accounts within your territory can be selected at your discretion (part of your Total Addressable Market (TAM)). I implore you to ensure that a portion/percentage of your target accounts are selected using the Sphere of Influence.

Develop your Sphere of Influence "Activation List" through visualization

As I previously mentioned, it's estimated that 85% of people are visual learners. You'll find account selection so much easier if you create a visual roadmap for yourself. Below is a diagram of a real-life scenario. We begin by placing a customer logo in the center of a sheet of paper. You might choose a specific company because it represents the best story you have in a territory, or the greatest brand recognition in a vertical. Don't get too hung up on identifying your first Sphere of Influence account, as you'll eventually learn to scale this throughout your entire customer base. Next, begin creating sections from that customer logo:

a. Past employees of that customer that are now key stakeholders in new companies that meet your Ideal Customer Profile (ICP) but are not current customers;
b. Competitors to your customer;
c. A list of key internal stakeholders within that account that have a high social proximity to your ICPs, and could refer you to that contact/company.

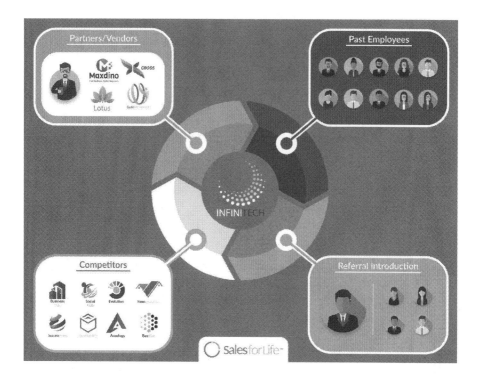

Step-by-step guide to Sphere of Influence account selection

Step 1: Choose an existing customer

As mentioned above, you should start by selecting an existing customer that can present a large opportunity base of new accounts. Here are examples of customers to focus on:

    a. Accounts with high churn (but great success with your solution). Key stakeholders that may have used your solution at that customer, and have moved on to become directors, vice-presidents and/or C-level executives in new companies;

    b. Accounts with large partner ecosystems. Focus on brands that are highly recognizable, and whose name would garner a new buyer's attention when used in future sales engagements;

    c. Highly competitive industries where even the mention of your customer's name will invoke engagement.

Step 2: Focus on existing customers – departed advocates

This sales play has created more opportunities and revenue for our customers than any other account selection action. These are the previous employees of your customer-base who move onto new companies. Some of these people are strong advocates for your solution, some were previous users, and some might only have heard a whisper of your company's name during their time of employment. One data study conducted by a customer of ours showed that the highest converting opportunities were their customer referrals at 68.7% – the exact reason to follow your advocates using the Sphere of Influence. At Sales for Life, in our fiscal year 2017, our "customer referral" opportunity source had a conversion of Sales Qualified Leads-to-Win at a 43% rate for mid-market and enterprise accounts, and 75% for small businesses! That's how powerful a potential advocate can be.

Your opportunity is clear. You need to reverse-engineer your customer's previous employees using LinkedIn (at the time of writing, LinkedIn Sales Navigator is the best source to use for this process). Your goal is to determine those who are in a position of power and have become a potential champion, influencer or decision-maker at a new account that meets your ICP. Using the Advanced Search criteria in LinkedIn Sales Navigator, search for your customer's accounts, while highlighting "Past not Current" (those people that no longer work at a specific company). Depending on your ICP, you'll need to continue filtering various fields such as industry, geography, company headcount, function and/or title. If the data is presenting you with too many LinkedIn profiles to review, you can filter by "years at current company" – in which I suggest selecting "less than 1 year". The rationale is that newly hired key stakeholders are more keen to bring change, and might possibly be keen to bring along the people, process and/or technology that made them successful in their past business... which is your solution!

Step 3: Map your existing accounts – competitors, partners and vendors

This step should seem very obvious to you. The most common Sphere of Influence sales play is identifying competitors to your customer base. In the digital sales era, there are so many sources for competitive information:

a. For public companies, leverage the Form 10-K of your customer, or known publicly-traded competitor to that customer, or other publicly-traded companies in your customer's vertical. The Form 10-K is simply described as the business plan that a publicly traded company publishes for shareholders to review. Everything you need will be published inside this document, including a list of competitors. Go to www.form10k.com to look up your customers, or companies in their vertical.

b. For private companies, we've seen sales professionals use all sorts of research tools, including Google Alerts, Dun & Bradstreet information, Glassdoor, Owler, Alexa, etc. The purpose here is to dig in and find all the companies that your customer is disrupting each day. Furthering your Sphere of Influence can also be achieved by identifying companies that sell to the same vertical or even buyer persona (job function within the company) as your existing customers. While they don't directly compete with your customer, they compete for mindshare and budgets. These companies see your customer at similar tradeshows and conferences, and may speak about them about in the office.

c. For partners and vendors, surf your customer's website for channel partners, alliances, vendors of record. These companies know your customer's name well, and their successes are intertwined.

Step 4: Social proximity of referral candidates

As I mentioned in my book *Social Selling Mastery®*,

> Aristotle's definition of synergy is "a whole greater than the sum of its parts". Social Selling (which is a component of a digital sales ecosystem) is a team sport. Depending on your role in the sales organization, you may not be connected with, or even really know, your existing customers.

You may not be 1st-degree LinkedIn connected with a vast majority of your existing customer base. That's fine, because someone in your organization should be. In many technology companies, that responsibility falls on Customer Success. In other industries, the role is tasked to Account Managers. Regardless of their function, each of your existing customers is made up of people, and those people have high social proximity to like-minded people (key stakeholders in other companies you want to do business with). Your mission as a sales **professional** ("professional" highlighted on purpose) is to NOT throw up your hands and say, "I don't know the customer success team", or "I don't think account managers have those connections".

Personally, if I were your sales leader, I wouldn't care for the excuses. You and I, as sales professionals, have a mission. That mission is to exceed sales quota attainment by selecting, engaging and winning accounts – PERIOD. I want to see sales professionals that have the drive and moxy to go organize the people that have the relationships with their customers or, if you have to, go seek out these relationships themselves. Sales quota attainment is on the line, and we're giving you're an asymmetrical competitive advantage that can leverage a customer relationship to broker sales opportunities for you! Locked inside your customer advocates are relationships that would take you a lifetime to access without any help. Use LinkedIn TeamLink (for internal relationship roadmapping) to help connect your entire sales organization together so you may centralize 1st-degree connection data. Your goal is to identify the following:

a. Which accounts are the most successful customers? Do I look for 'Power users'? Net Promoter Scores? Recency effect (still in the 'honeymoon period' with our company)?
b. Who are the champions, influencers and decision-makers that my internal team speaks with consistently inside our customer-base?
c. Are any of these customer advocates already open to being a referral broker without having to ask their permission in advance? If not, what would be protocol for approaching these customer advocates?

Don't limit your options to only the customer advocates that your team really likes and deals with all the time. Push your team to recognize the amplifying effects of extending their social proximity range. We suggest road mapping all the champions, influencers and decision-makers in an account, and align your thinking with the book *The Challenger Customer*, which models an average number of key stakeholders in an account as 7.4 people. If your team is not personally connected to all these potential referral brokers (advocates in your customer base) on LinkedIn, have a candid conversation with your team about who will approach each customer to ensure a 1st-degree LinkedIn connection. Be crystal-clear with your team on the engagement process, so you're not bombarding the same customer with referrals. Best-in-class sales professionals will take a moment to reach out to each customer and explain their new "Sphere of Influence" referral sales process. We find that few customers will object.

Which accounts and connections have the highest social proximity to my customer-base?
Once you begin to master LinkedIn and reverse-engineering your customers' social networks, the possibilities really start to amplify. You're able to open the 1st-degree LinkedIn connections of every customer advocate and see their entire social network. This exercise can bring you down a rabbit hole. The spider-web of possibilities becomes infinite, your mouth begins to salivate as you mentally calculate the Total Addressable Market (TAM), but then you have a quick panic: "Someone actually has to contact all these people. Where do I start?" Remember that focus and time management are both your allies and your enemies.

TIP: Focus on the first five accounts that an advocate has the highest social proximity to.

Inside your advocate's 1st-degree LinkedIn network might be 500, 1000, 5000 connections. Logically you can conduct a search within their social network for a specific ICP, such as "VP Sales" or "Chief Executive Officer", which is relatively helpful. There will be prospective buyers in that list. But to get a really clear picture of an advocate's highest social proximity we must recognize that when people have strong relationships at an account, typically they have more than one connection in that account. In fact, they most likely have many, many connections. Perhaps they used to work at that company, or their best friend works there and their social networks have converged for after-work drinks, or they've been a vendor/partner to your advocate for a few years. Focus your time on the five accounts that your advocate really has deep relationships with, and your assumption (which will regularly hold true) that high social connections in an account have a correlation to high social proximity. Think of this as an asymmetrical competitive advantage that has provided you a higher "propensity to buy" score.

Chapter 4: The Activation List operating framework

"Simplicity is the ultimate sophistication."

Leonardo Da Vinci

In the months that I've been writing this book, I've noticed an alarming trend. Whether I'm more attuned to the problem or it's becoming more pervasive, I'm not really sure. The problem is simple: sales professionals are neither thinking nor acting like they're the CEO of their own territory. These sales professionals are approaching their territories with the same rigor that my four-year-old daughter applies herself to cleaning her room... which is **no focus at all**. Yes, these sales professionals have lists, and yes, they're creating sales actions in the market, but they don't appear to have the same structured thinking that a CEO is required to use when developing a business plan. One of the most basic fundamentals of developing a business plan for investors is logically outlining the Total Addressable Market (TAM) of a territory/market/industry. There is no business plan worth reading if the CEO can't articulate the TAM of the market.

Step 1: Logically outline the TAM of your territory
For account-based sales professionals that have been assigned a set number of accounts, with an Activation List that can not fluctuate or change (their TAM is pre-defined), this exercise may not be applicable. If this pertains to you, I still recommend you learn this skill regardless, as this business planning structure may be hyper-valuable to you in the future. The goal of this exercise is to understand the size of a particular market opportunity, measured in account units. No, it's not just the responsibility of your C-level executives or sales operations to know this information. This is YOUR territory, and as CEO of that territory you have the responsibility! Using tools such as LinkedIn, or data sources such as Seamless.ai, ZoomInfo, DiscoverOrg, Dun & Bradstreet, etc.,

combined with your internal CRM databases, I recommend you map the following:

a. Which accounts are now/have been customers in some capacity?

    i. Existing/Active customers
    ii. Passive customers (such as pay-per-usage that's unpredictable)
    iii. Inactive/Dormant customers

b. Which accounts then remain prospective customers and opportunities?

    i. Activated prospective accounts (accounts that have had sales opportunities created by yourself, or someone else in your organization – selling into that account)
    ii. Non-Activated prospective accounts (have yet to have conversations with)

STEP #1 - TAM Mapping

Segment your Total Addressable Market by type of customer and prospective account. **This is your baseline.**

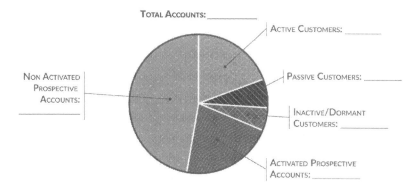

The results of this exercise become your baseline. From that baseline, we need to establish a logical account selection list (Activation List) that aligns to your lead/opportunity creation requirements, highly influencing your ability to meet sales quota. Finally, we have to set milestones along a timeline that help you accomplish your goal of:

a. Shrinking the number of non-activated prospective accounts, turning them into activated prospective accounts, and eventually customers;

b. Always being accountable for having a Activation List of prospective accounts organized and ready for engagement. This means the Activation List size (X number of accounts) will highly influence your sales quota attainment.

TERRITORY DEVELOPMENT:
Total Addressable Market (TAM) vs. Activated Accounts

Step #2 - My Required Targeted Account List

Reverse-engineer your required pipeline coverage
of accounts to achieve sale quota attainment.
This is your goal.

How many accounts (in units) would you need to win, in a calendar year, to achieve
sales quota attainment?
ie. Sales Quota / ACV (Average Contact Value)

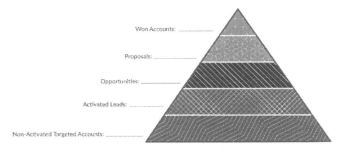

Won Accounts: _____

Proposals: _____

Opportunities: _____

Activated Leads: _____

Non-Activated Targeted Accounts: _____

Step 2: Use structured thinking to solve for (X number of accounts)

This is exactly where we see sales professionals, and their sales leadership, either develop a highly structured account plan, or allow their sales professionals to wander around their territory aimlessly. I like to believe I've heard and seen everything. I've heard:

"I don't know."

"It doesn't matter, I just need sales."

"50 accounts" (when the math clearly indicated that number to be woefully insufficient)

"1,000 accounts" (when the conversion rates of this "shotgun approach" are so low you can't understand why there isn't a higher level of account concentration)

45

"100 accounts" (and when you probe further, the sales leader says "I chose that number because it *felt* manageable")

Again I want us to come back to the idea of being the CEO of your territory. Imagine I was finalizing a presentation to our commercial bank. In our pitch for tripling our line of credit, allowing Sales for Life to improve our access to capital, the Vice-president of Commercial Lending asks me in the meeting: "Jamie, how many accounts will each of your sales professionals target, and what percentage of those accounts will you expect them to turn into opportunities?" With a bewildered look on my face, I say: "I think each sales professional should target 100 accounts because I think they could manage that workload day-to-day". The banker gives me a funny look and says: "I'm not concerned about their workload, I'm focused on your ability to create scalable lead flow so that you have the accounts receivables necessary to cover this expanded line of credit – that's your sales objective!" I recognize this example is extreme, but it highlights the point of thinking like a CEO of a territory. Activation List requirements are a **science**, not an art.

a.   Gather data – the three levers of sales performance
As a sales professional, you have three main levers to draw upon during your sales process: volumes, velocity (time) and probability/conversions. The only way to develop an account list with proper structured thinking is with data. Whether you already have this data in your CRM, or need to have a roundtable with sales/marketing operations, or just need to "guesstimate," data will help you reverse-engineer for the common denominator. You're looking for the best flow of data you can find on the following:

- To win one account, how many X (contracts, proposals, opportunities) do we typically require?
- How long, on average, does it take to work an account from 'Stage X' to won account?

Remember this book is a guide, not a university textbook, so we can't gobble up chapters on mathematical equations. But I hope I've illustrated the point enough to allow you to move to the next step.

b. Reverse-engineer the data down to one number: opportunities

You're essentially trying to solve for one number. My number at Sales for Life is called a "Sales Qualified Lead" (SQL). I know the following from our fiscal year 2018:

- The average velocity (time) from SQL-to-Win for our product "Social Selling Mastery®" is 57 days, and the median is 30 days.
- For all account-based SQLs created (professional-driven outbound sales), we win 47%.

Using the one basic formula that SQL = 47% conversion in 57 days (rounded simply as 50% in 60 days), I can then set a very definite goal for future SQL creation. The challenge we see in most sales organizations is that sales leadership may have a strong enough handle on "that number", but haven't thought to look beyond that number to understand the actions and activities required to generate "that number".

c. Continue reverse-engineering the data down to one number: activations

This is the most critical element that's constantly overlooked. How many activated accounts (we call those 'Sales Accepted Leads', or SALs, at Sales for Life) does a sales professional need to be working on at any given time in order to create "that number"? You are looking deeper into the activities of your sales professionals – for conversation starters, first meetings, coffee dates, discovery calls, phone calls, LinkedIn chat conversations, etc. You are thinking about the number of conversations a sales professional is having to reach one unit (SALs converting into one opportunity or SQL). Now you must extrapolate your Sales Accepted Lead (SAL) unit numbers, to highly influence your ultimate goal – sales quota attainment.

At Sales for Life, each of our teammates knows "their number". As an example, a teammate requires 50 SQLs per year to highly influence achieving sales quota attainment. Within those 50 SQLs, there is a percentage assumed from our five SQL sources (Inbound, Outbound account-based from sales professional (ABSD), Channel, Customer Referral, Customer Expansion). In our fiscal year 2019, our team knows that each sales professional is required to deliver 10 SQLs from outbound account-based efforts (as part of their 50 SQLs). So 10 is their goal! Consequently, we can work backwards to see how they can achieve this goal:

- 10 SQLs is the goal
- 50% of Activations (SALs) convert into a SQL
- 20 SALs are thus required
- 20% of Non-Activated accounts from an Activation List (examples are coffee meetings, LinkedIn chats, phone conversations, etc. – accounts we do not have active sales cycles in yet) convert into SAL
- 100 Non-Activated accounts in the Activation List is thus required

Stop and think about what these figures mean. This means that each teammate at Sales for Life requires a Activation List of >100 accounts, or the probability they'll achieve their goal is diminished. What it also means is that each teammate is focused on a number that they can control. It's not arbitrary, it's simple math!

d. Map sales velocity to adjust your Activation List requirements

For some sales organizations, or sales professionals (such as enterprise sales professionals), there is one major variable that will affect their Activation List: Sales Cycle Timelines. At Sales for Life, I know that on average new accounts will cycle in or out of our Activation Cycle within one quarter. This helps us adjust our Activation List requirements accordingly.

Best-in-class organizations take a moment with their sales operations team to conduct this analysis. They factor in average sales cycle velocities to their Activation List requirements. A real-life example is where our customers have enterprise sales professionals working accounts with an average contract value

(ACV) of >$1,000,000 USD. These transactions take nine to 24 months to materialize. What these best-in-class sales teams do is factor in the average timelines it would take to:

1. Activate one account into a conversation
2. Turn those conversations into an opportunity
3. Turn an opportunity into a customer

From there, they reverse-engineer the sales professionals' $3 million, $5 million, or perhaps $15 million sales quota into a number they can control. How many accounts does this sales professional need to be moving from non-activated to activated account THIS YEAR, in order to have opportunities NEXT YEAR?

Step 3: Develop a Service Level Agreement (SLA) between sales leaders and sales professionals on adhering to Activation List accountability

How specifically do best-in-class sales organizations maintain consistent sales pipeline creation? With accountability measures! It's that simple and sophisticated. These organizations have completely integrated their Activation List requirements into a sales professional's one-on-ones with their sales leaders. They have done this because *their number* is so simple, and directly correlated to being a leading indicator to sales success. The sales professional is not left to their own devices, and there are definitely no "random acts" of account selection. As CEO of my territory, there's no way I'm going to leave my sales goals to chance. Every sales professional has *their number* that they can control and align to.

TARGET ACCOUNT SELECTION - TARGET LIST ACCOUNTABILLITY TEMPLATE

○ salesforLife™

What accounts are you targeting to activate using the "Sphere of Influence"?

Notes: Explain why you've selected these accounts and how you'll engage the account.

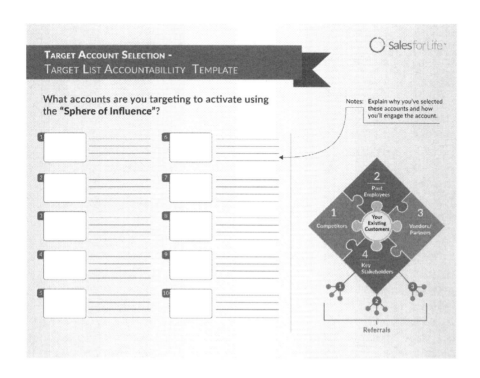

50

Chapter 5: Sphere of Influence complementing existing sales territory plans

"Never stop testing, and your advertising will never stop improving."

David Ogilvy

You're leaving a work event after a night of fun, and you need to get home. Less than ten years ago, your main option was to find a taxi. You could walk to a cab stand, wave your arms around frantically in the street, or, in some cities, call the cab company with a fixed address. Today there are more options: Uber, Lyft, and dozens of competitors that pop up every year. The transportation industry has evolved dramatically. Your friends would think you were insane if you said to them: "John, my mission is to get home. But I've always found taxis by whistling and jumping up and down. I'm not going to use my mobile phone to hail an Uber because it seems like an extra step." Uber and Lyft are simply mechanisms that have made life easier, as a **complement** to your mission of getting home. Your buyer has evolved more in the last ten years than in the previous hundred years. The modern, digital sales professional does not treat digital activities as separate initiatives from their more traditional activities. They don't see Uber and separate for taxis, they only see Uber as a mechanism for achieving a result. They don't see digital innovation as "alien", "foreign" or "additional", they see these activities as complementary.

Regardless of your territory plan – whether it's geographic, verticalized by industry, and/or buyer persona-driven by role/function – there are always complementary data points that can help you focus. Your goal is to achieve sales quota attainment by focusing on the accounts that have the highest propensity to buy. Without you having deep artificial intelligence capabilities, I highly recommend you complement your account selection process with the best data you have available: the asymmetrical competitive advantage of social proximity you and your existing customers have around relationships.

As a sales leader, you might be reading this and thinking: "I completely see how one sales professional leverages the Sphere of Influence as a complement to their account selection process, but I have 10 sales professionals (or 100, or 1,000)! How can this work without disrupting our current territory alignment?" This is an important question, as changing your territory alignment is not my purpose here. The goal is to better equip your sales professionals to perform within their existing frameworks. Our best-in-class customers have tackled the scalability of Sphere of Influence account selection with three approaches:

Model A: Centralized data control and disbursement of target lists

Model B: Decentralized territory control at the sales professional level

Model C: Fair enterprise with social proximity

Model A: Centralized data control and disbursement of target lists

I'll fully admit that I'm not a big fan of this model. I think the reason is not due to lack of effectiveness, but the risk it poses for sales professionals in their territories. This model requires the centralization of digital data and insights collection (typically conducted by lead generation/sales support functions) to mine data points such as job change alerts, news alerts, job postings, social connections for referrals etc., and distribute these insights out to the applicable sales professionals in that territory.

You know that saying "give a person a fish and you feed him for a day; teach them to fish and you feed them for a lifetime"? This is the equivalent to handing out food to the sales professionals. You're not teaching the sales professional to fish on their own. If the "taps" of this centralized model were ever to turn off, would the sales professionals have the skills and capabilities to "fish" on their own? I think it's a hindrance to the type of sales culture you're probably trying to build. Yet there are companies that run this model with great effectiveness, because they view the problem-to-solution as simple unit economics: have the $100/hour resources doing $100/hour tasks, while the $15/hour resources conduct $15/hour tasks. I'd argue that these skills are not a commodity but a strategic advantage for the sales professionals. However, some companies see only the output, and assign time and materials to that labor accordingly. In practice, the model may look something like this:

    a. Inside sales/sales support mines data for job change alerts on LinkedIn in a group of cities;
    b. Once job change alerts are activated, the data team cross-references the key stakeholders on that list against their internal CRM, and checks the validity of the data;
    c. The list is purged down to the most relevant leads, and prepared in a spreadsheet or inputted into the CRM for the Monday "all-hands call";
    d. On Monday, the sales organization reviews the data of the new key accounts the sales team should target based on high social proximity.

Model B: Decentralized territory control at the sales professional level

The teacher in me likes this model better, as it places control in the hands of the sales professional. Personally, as a sales professional, I wish that social tools like LinkedIn (along with my developed skills to leverage LinkedIn) had been in my sales toolkit 10 years ago. My recommendation is to start small, and then A/B test. A/B testing is also important if you're trying to build a business case for any long-term change management to the territory development plans. Using the Target List Accountability template I shared earlier, start with ten accounts within a territory. Using those, prove that targeting high social proximity accounts does the following:

    a. Shorten the Activation Cycle
    b. Increase the ability to activate an account

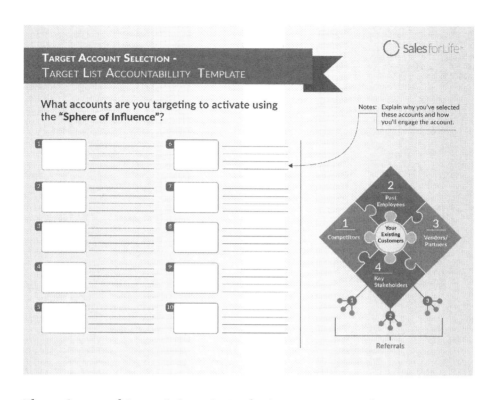

What accounts are you targeting to activate using the **"Sphere of Influence"**?

Notes: Explain why you've selected these accounts and how you'll engage the account.

The only way this model works in the long term is with buy-in and accountability driven from front-line sales leaders. By taking the responsibility out of the hands of one single leader (Model A might report to the Director of Demand Generation, VP Marketing, or Vice-President of Inside Sales, for example), this decentralized model is far more complex from a change management perspective. You need a collective feedback mechanism to ensure that:

    a. Sales professionals are leveraging this account selection process;

    b. Front-line sales leaders are overseeing and ensuring the accountability of this plan;

    c. You (if you're a Chief Revenue Officer or similar reading this) are communicating the results effectively, and holding your front-line sales leaders accountable to change management.

Model C: Fair enterprise with social proximity

This model is effective for:

    a. SMB companies that have "green fields" of opportunity (more opportunity than their salesforce could possibly manage),

    b. Entrepreneurial businesses such as professional services firms (companies where sales professionals manage "clients" from lead to client to implementation/delivery),

    c. Highly collaborative/partner-centric organizations.

This model is a hybrid of a common territory model, but allows social proximity to supersede territories. The reason this is allowed is... **sales results** – delivered in any way you can achieve the goal (which is, after all, the ultimate goal). Think asymmetrical competitive advantages superseding traditional structure.

Here is a real-life example of a collaborative/partner-centric model. Jill Rowley was a quota-crushing machine at Eloqua (in the days before Eloqua was acquired by Oracle). One of her favorite digital sales plays was leveraging the social proximity of her university, the University of Virginia. She would call, email, text message or tweet fellow alumni that had gone on to be C-level executives, and she would open her conversations with "Wah-hoo-wah" (the football battle cry at the school). This approach was highly successful and opened her eyes to all sorts of possibilities. Jill realized that she was socially connected to many CMOs and CEOs of companies outside her designated territory, so she partnered with the sales professionals of other territories to create the necessary introductions, activating accounts, sharing in the sales deliverables (workload), and collecting 50% of the deal. This was a win/win/win for everyone:

    a. Jill earned opportunities based on logical relationships she could tap into;

    b. The sales professional in that territory gained a new account in their market, and 50% of something they never had before;

    c. The organization gained a new client, with no additional Cost of Customer Acquisition (CAC).

You can obviously see how breaking down the territory silos in a SMB business makes sense (we don't care who's talking to who – just win us more deals). You can also see that in entrepreneurial environments like professional services companies, your competition is both outside and inside the organization. Accounts are stolen from internal teammates all the time (I came from commercial real estate and investment advisory, where this is common practice). Obviously, this model is not without its challenges, as it needs collaboration/partner-centric mindsets to foster adoption. If your organization is a lone-wolf's den, then forget about it. This model is optimal for companies that are collectively looking out for the best interests of the organization (a goal like capital raises, IPO, aggressive sales targets) rather than the loss/sharing of an account in a territory. If everyone thought and acted like the "CEO of a territory", what would you do as a CEO?

a. **Gain buy-in:** "The whole is greater than the sum of its parts," says Aristotle. We are going to gobble up market share more rapidly with this complementary model. As a sales professional I might find opportunities based on my current relationships that I can activate outside my territory (as a secondary focus), while at the same time being brought into opportunities that frankly I would have struggled to activate on my own.

b. **Document a plan:** I need to think about rules of engagement. I want this to be a complementary activity (more like secondary effort within a territory), so what percentage mix of accounts can/should my team share? What is the Service Level Agreement between these sales professionals, so that we continue to maximize the customer experience? What is the collective compensation model? What is the dispute resolution process? Can sales professionals swap and trade accounts for 100% ownership, or do we keep a 50%/50% sharing model?

c. **Communicate the plan:** Change doesn't happen after one single email. How do I ensure everyone understands exactly how this plan works? Where do they go for additional questions and resources? How can we improve our sales professionals' skills in "collaborative selling", so that we maximize the client experience?

d. **Ensure accountability to the plan:** As the CEO, you want results. The details behind the scenes are less important than the results. It's only when the results are less effective than expected, or the system is frankly broken, that you get frustrated and jump into the details. Anticipate those challenges up front by assigning accountability to this new model. How are sales leaders acting in the company's best interest by assigning account projects to the people with the highest social proximity to the account? This is a critical step that I've seen Chief Revenue Officers and/or Chief Executive Officers take. They think customer-centric first, and then reverse-engineer the customer like they're thinking about sales professionals as chess pieces. Which chess piece on this key account can give us an asymmetrical competitive advantage based on their high social proximity to the account?

PART 2: PLAN your sales plays with storyboards

Chapter 6: Storyboarding: the power of visualizing your buyer's journey

"The only thing worse than being blind is having sight with no vision."
Helen Keller

In the early 1930s a famous animation and motion picture producer named Walt Disney changed how movies were created. In the creation of Three Little Pigs in 1933, the team used Walt's comic-book like sketches (which he had tried before in 1928 with Steamboat Willie) to visualize the entire motion picture. This was a revelation, as it dramatically reduced planning, developing and editing time. Now all stakeholders on a project could see where the story was going.

Of course these days this is standard operating procedure in all movies. Can you imagine the director calling all the acting talent onto the set without a clear visual plan for the shot, only to waste millions of dollars that day just trying to work out what happens next in the movie? The original definition of a storyboard is "a graphic organizer in the form of illustrations or images displayed in sequence for the purpose of pre-visualizing a motion picture, animation, motion graphic or interactive media sequence". This definition has broadened as software developers, advertising agencies, and scientific researchers use the same process.

Here is a common problem I see over and over with sales and marketing organizations. The sales team says to us "we don't know what to say when we engage the customer". Or, they might have a seven-touch email cadence mapped into their sales engagement software (such as Salesloft or Outreach.io), but when you read what's being sent to prospective customers, there is no real value in their messages. You'll have seen this yourself when you receive a series of unsolicited emails from companies, and you realize that their last three messages seemed eerily similar. Inside that sales organization, it's as though the movie director (sales leader) has walked onto the set (the sales floor) and said: "OK team, we're just going to improvise today. You just 'act' and I'll record everything." There is clearly no plan at all. If the concept of storyboarding is so widely used in other fields, why are sales and marketing teams not stepping back and designing both initial sales plays (early scenes in a movie) and learning paths (acts 2 and 3 in the motion picture) for your customers?

The benefits of this process are very compelling, and certainly squash any detractors' objections of "we don't have time for this" (unfortunately I typically hear this excuse from marketing).

1. **Massive time/cost savings at scale**: I'd like you to put your CFO hat on for a moment. Let's take a look at your sales team, using one inside sales professional at $50,000/year salary and one account executive at $100,000/year salary as our examples. Countless time management and productivity studies on sales professionals show shockingly low levels of direct selling time per week. I won't use these, as I'll make it simpler. There are 2,000 business hours a year, so the inside sales professional makes $25/hour salary, and the account executive makes $50/hour. Let's assume these sales professionals spend two hours a week developing their own sales plays (a round number of 100 man-hours per sales professional, per year). If each week the sales professionals are "lost and cobbling together garbage" in their sales messaging, and lack a compelling sales play for each touch-point:

Direct cost (wastage):

- Inside sales professional = $2,500/year
- Account Executive = $5,000/year

Let's assume that the expected sales quota attainment for each of these sales professionals is five times their OTE (On Target Earnings).

Opportunity cost (at risk from time not in the field from 100 man-hours):

- Inside sales professional = $12,500/year of lost sales
- Account Executive = $25,000/year of lost sales

As CFO, you recognize that on your sales team of 100 Account Executives, the scaling impact of $500,000/year direct cost ($5,000 x 100 sales professionals) has also placed $2,500,000/year ($25,000 x 100 sales professionals) at risk for opportunity sales cost. This is unacceptable! But sales teams do this every day by not taking one step backwards to plan and storyboard highly compelling and digitally-rich sales plays that will empower sales professionals and engage customers.

2. **Centralize sales play design (think AGILE or SCRUM development process):** In a movie, there are so many stakeholders – actors, directors, producers, sound/lighting, editors, etc. If the actor (using our analogy for a sales professional) doesn't like something in storyboard and script, there is a centralized editing and communication process, so everyone downstream in the movie production cycle can adjust. In software development, you can have multiple teams working on multiple projects, all centralizing their ideas to work towards a much bigger project (read about AGILE or SCRUM for more on this). Where sales and marketing communication often fails is when the sales professional can clearly see customer messages that have failed or succeeded, but has no mechanism for communicating this to their leaders, marketing or peers. Best-in-class teams realize that some storyboarded sales plays will hit the mark, and some sales plays will fail to resonate with customers. EVERYONE in the sales and marketing organization needs to know what works and what fails. You, as a sales professional, need a clear line of communication to see storyboards that are in

development, and storyboards that are available for customer distribution today.

In my first book, *Social Selling Mastery®*, I discussed the sales and marketing alignment process called "IP (Intellectual Property) Transfer Loop". This sales process, which is used to develop content marketing assets like blogs, webinars and infographics, is the same internal process needed to develop storyboards. The sales and marketing team can collaborate on what topics are important, trending, and really pushing buyers off their status quo. That valuable data can then be shared via finalized sales plays (an example is a designed LinkedIn PointDrive, storing these assets in Team Presentations for community access by all sales professionals), which we'll cover in future chapters.

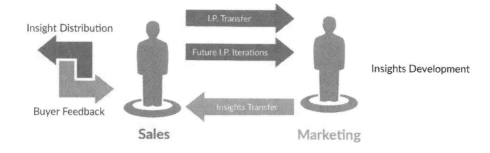

3. **Scale success once you hit on the right message:** Nothing feels more gratifying to a sales professional than finding a sales rhythm. It's exhilarating when you've agonized over how to make your sales process more efficient, and manage to craft a sales message (whether that's a phone, email, social, video or live presentation) that hits the mark. Given time, either you or someone in your sales organization is bound to "strike gold". Someone will find a topic and message that really reaches to the core of your buyers' challenges. By having a centralized storyboarding process, you can deploy this successful message to your sales peers so they can rapidly adjust. Storyboarding sales plays allows

you to pivot messages quickly for speed-to-market execution.

4. **Mitigate the risk of rogue messaging:** Marketing teams have been trying to curb this challenge for years in organizations. This problem will never completely disappear, but you can discourage it through centralized sales plays. Find something that works and your sales professionals will have no interest in spending their time individually designing their own sales plays, as they can more easily pull from existing templates, only slightly contextualizing/tailoring the play for a particular account. You are now creating one voice in the market!

Chapter 7: War Room: design prescriptive sales plays within an engagement framework

"A goal without a plan is just a wish."
Antoine de Saint-Exupéry

Sales and marketing alignment is critical in the planning of your storyboarded sales plays. But you as a sales professional can also work autonomously, and be highly successful. Digital sales technology has evolved to become more sales-centric, allowing the sales professional to act as both the sales professional and the marketer (known as "micro-marketing"). This is fantastic for anyone within a small business, or those sales professionals that just can't garner the attention of marketing. In speaking to sales leaders, I do however want to concentrate this chapter on the assumption that sales and marketing are willing to become better dance partners. This alignment will be a game-changer for your business!

Step 1: Form an Insights Committee
In my first book, *Social Selling Mastery®*, I discuss the definition and design of this committee. For your benefit, I'll summarize it. Your Insights Committee is a small selection of sales professionals that come together, either live or virtually, on a regular basis (typically monthly) to brainstorm content ideas. These ideas are formulated from real-life sales interactions with customers – their objections, pitfalls, challenges, market concerns, stories from the road, etc. The purpose of the Insights Committee is to gain:

    a. Deeper intellectual property for content/insights based on frontline experiences, not just marketing's subjective feel for customer sentiment;

b. Greater content engagement from the sales team, both in the creation and the distribution process. Sales professionals will share content THEY create;

c. A tight feedback loop of new ideas that surface from customers discussing the content that sales professionals distribute. Based on that customer feedback, a new or improved version of the story can be created.

Best practice has Insights Committees of five to eight sales professionals, drawn together from various functions or business units. This helps you gather ideas from several sources: lead generation, account management, solution consulting, channel partners, etc.

Step 2: Focus on one customer type to develop a storyboard framework
In running these Insights Committee meetings, we will typically draw a buyer persona on a whiteboard, give that buyer personal a name (to make it seem real), and focus the entire meeting (typically an hour) on that person. What you're trying to create is a template for all future storyboards, so that you can create derivatives of your original process (by language, localized by market, by vertical, etc.).

GET CUSTOMER-CENTRIC – think from the customer's mindset outward. This is not an exercise in thinking about how your solutions align to customer problems, which defeats the purpose of the exercise. Go around the room and ensure that each sales professional has a voice, and ask one simple question to each sales professional, that they must write down (on a whiteboard or sticky note) for later discussion:

"What is the number one question you hear from your customers each day?"

Focus on their problems, remembering that the problems your customer faces are not necessarily ones that your solution solves. Think of their overarching business challenges.

Step 3: Vote on a key problem, and double-click as a team
As your Insights Committee fields all the ideas from the team, vote on which is the most relevant, most common question that continues to emerge. This will be your focal-point. Now, as a team, begin openly talking about that problem:

1. How often are you hearing about this problem?
2. When during the buying journey is this problem surfacing?
3. On a scale of 1-5, how critical is solving this problem for our customers?
4. On a scale of 1-5, how critical is answering some or all of their questions about this problem in order to move forward with a purchase decision?
5. How many stakeholders in a customer's organization does this problem affect? Who are those other stakeholders?
6. How is this problem originally created? Internal inefficiencies? External macro-economic forces?
7. How have your customer's competitors solved this problem?

There are endless directions in which you can take your discovery questions. The purpose here is to place yourself in your customer's shoes, and really begin thinking through the questions that will need answering.

Step 4: Organize ideas logically for structured sales plays
You're still in planning mode, but now you're starting to think about the arrangement of your problem-solving ideas. Some of the best Insights Committee meetings I've been a part of have moved towards a role-playing exercise. This is where one person in the room (perhaps marketing) plays the customer, while the other sales professionals logically think through the order of operations of ideas, facts, data sheets, network connections, live events, etc. that a customer would need to best absorb ideas and to better solve their problem. Best-in-class teams will not limit their thinking to the content assets, networking events and data intelligence that they have access to **today**. As I'll outline in further chapters, best-in-class teams will use these insights to invent assets, events or data intelligence that will become the compelling center-pieces to their customer engagement. At this stage, think with an open mind and organize your ideas in an order of operations that mirrors how a customer would logically structure their thinking. This is likely to change and develop: the one certainty about buyers is that the buying journey is often not linear. All you can do is **try** to create a logical process for buyers that will best help them on their buying journey.

Step 5: War Room your account as a Data Intelligence Briefing
In 2017, we began a series of global Social Selling Mastery® projects with Teleperformance. To date, I have yet to meet a more sophisticated account planning company. Their Average Contract Value (ACV) is millions of dollars, with sales cycles that are 12–36 months. Each sales professional needs to hyper–focus on planning and executing a highly valuable engagement strategy for their customers. Teleperformance took this process literally, planning key accounts on sheets of paper in a boardroom (like a war room), and later turning this process into a Data Intelligence Brief (via PDF) for each key account. If an account is key to your customer's sales pipeline (such as 'Top 10' or 'Strategic 25', the account needs to be 'War Roomed'). This elegantly simple, yet highly valuable, exercise has changed how account–based sales professionals engage their customers.

What is the War Room?
It's a visual roadmap of your strategic engagement strategy for one account. Using the power of visualization, you plan your "go-to-market" in this one account, based on the four pillars of Digital Selling: Triggers, Referrals, Insights and Competitive Intelligence.

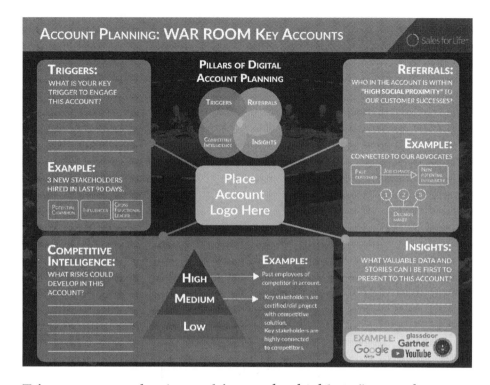

Triggers – external or internal factors that highly influence change in a customer. Examples of key triggers:

- Executive job changes
- Company expansion and retraction
- Technology integrations that match your customer's "tech stack"
- A customer's competition launches a product, or finalizes a large investment
- A customer launches a new product
- A customer invests heavily in key markets/marketing (such as industry sponsorships)

Best-in-class sales organizations will leverage free and/or paid tools to gather the intelligence necessary to build a Data Intelligence Brief on an account. Example free tools are: Google Alerts, Built With, AngelList, VisualPing, Crunchbase, Glassdoor, Owler, IFTTT, Twitter.

Referrals – your ability to leverage your social network, your colleagues' social networks, or your customers' social networks, to be brokered introductions to key stakeholders in the account. You are leveraging key learnings from Chapter 3, by using your Sphere of Influence process to look for high social proximity connections and referral opportunities.

Competitive Intelligence – you are looking for asymmetrical competitive *disadvantages* in an account.

- Highest Risk – previous employees of your competitors are now employees in your account, and have senior leadership roles/can influence the buying committee.
- Medium Risk – key stakeholders in your account clearly showcasing skills, certifications and/or projects from your competitors on their LinkedIn profiles.
- Medium Risk – as you connect to key stakeholders on LinkedIn in your account, you notice they are well connected to your competition on LinkedIn as well.

All of these factors should be reviewed with sales leadership. What is the opportunity cost of engaging this account, rather than focusing elsewhere? Are we going to "spin our wheels" for six months, only to find out we're not going to win their business anyway because of competitive intelligence variables?

Insights – sales teams have two paths for insights: created by marketing, or curated from third-party sources. In Chapter 8, we begin discussing how we gather insights that tell incredible stories for your customers. You can source insights from Twitter, Glassdoor, Google Alerts, YouTube, www.form10k.com, research firms like Gartner, Forrester, IDC, Frost & Sullivan, etc. The purpose is to find insights that resonate and rock your customers off their status quo.

Your War Room is a Data Intelligence Briefing that can be summarized on one-page, and presented to sales leadership in your one-on-ones. Each sales leader in your organization has a clear outline of the focal points for each key account, and can leverage this process as a current indicator of strong sales behavior and accountability, which will highly influence positive sales objectives.

Chapter 8: Sales play 1 – The Sphere of Influence connection

"People don't buy goods and services. They buy relationships, stories and magic."
Seth Godin

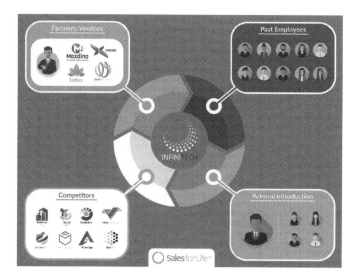

In the next five chapters, I'll outline five of the most popular sales plays that our customers have been deploying with great success, along with the overarching themes for these sales plays. In Part 3 of this book we'll further discuss the tools, events and/or communication mediums used to execute each sales play.

I use the Sphere of Influence sales play first, more obviously if this account was selected using the Sphere of Influence. This means that I've chosen to activate this account because it fits my ICP and has a high social proximity to successes my company has already had.

Basically, I reverse-engineer all the companies and social networks of our customer base for Asymmetrical Competitive Advantages.

This storyboard should be quite straightforward. I share direct stories of people and/or companies that the buyer will immediately find compelling. There is no randomness to my "name dropping". Similarly, I'll use a storyboard to share a connection between a current customer and the prospective customer that's bridged by a common relationship to success. In this way I'll humanize myself and demonstrate that we're only a 1st-degree connection away from each other. People buy trust, and that's what I'm trying to bridge: "You can trust me as I'm really close to your business's trusted sources".

Chapter 9: Sales Play 2 – Stack-ranking the account vs. competition vs. best-in-class

"All successful companies are constantly benchmarking their competition. They have to know what they have to match up with day-in and day-out if their company is going to be successful."

James Dunn

We find, and our customers find, that this data-centric approach is a great wake-up call. As a prime example, Gartner's Magic Quadrant rankings are an excellent example of this sales play. You're delivering data to a customer to help them understand their market position against their direct competition, and/or best-in-class.

Here are examples of sources that we and our customers have leveraged:

- Analyst groups like Gartner, Frost & Sullivan, Forrester, SiriusDecisions, Info-Tech Research Group and IDC
- Crowdsourced data sites like Glassdoor, Owler, TripAdvisor, etc.
- Financial sites that use SEC filings (Form 10-K) for financial performance, or government agencies

The purpose here is to push the buyer off their status quo by helping them recognize that others in the market are exceeding their benchmark, and help them question why they aren't making similar changes. One customer of ours that uses this effectively is Hughes Networks, a global leader in satellite and internet services. Its customer base covers a range of sectors, but it has a strong foundation in retail, petroleum retail and QSR (quick-serve restaurants), among others. Rather than rely on third-party data, the company creates its own data by conducting in-depth store audits and walkthroughs, interviewing customers, and even leveraging the data from mobile phone traffic patterns within the retailer. Hughes Networks can help their clients predict traffic volumes, tendencies, and buying habits in their customer base. Armed with this knowledge, they can help the entire petroleum retail industry understand what best-in-class looks like.

- How many people should walk through your store on a Sunday?
- How long should they stay?
- What should their average spend be?
- What feedback do customers have about your in-store wi-fi?

This is helping your prospective customers recognize their SWOT: Strengths, Weaknesses, Opportunities, and Threats.

Chapter 10: Sales Play 3 – Market Intelligence and Trends

> "Companies that get in trouble have a failure to see two realities: market trends and competitor attacks."
>
> – Michael J. Silverstein

Let's help push your customer to another learning level by showing them the future – pontification. The goal here is to present the customer with a crystal ball view into the future. Showcase where the market is moving and provide ideas, based on futuristic trends, that they need to be concerned with today.

The reality is that most customers live in a bubble. I live in a bubble, too. I've found over my last six years as a CEO that I've grown so focused on digital selling best practices that I hadn't been developing my financial acumen around the professional services industry at the same pace. I'm recently learning now (six years into the business) what the benchmark of CAGR (Compound Annual Growth Rate) expectation is for the sales performance/sales training industry. The truth is that we can't know everything, we can't learn everything… that's why we buy solutions.

For this sales play, think like you're running the Consumer Electronics Show in Las Vegas, Nevada each year. This show is a look into the future. Your sales play will also reach into the future. HOT TREND: right now, we're seeing many of our customers focus their sales plays on the year 2020 (this book is written in 2018).

- What will their growth rates, EBITA, market potential, and expected market share look like in 2025?
- How will your ecosystem morph by 2025?
- What tools, platforms, and systems are companies beta testing right now that will be standard operating procedures in 2025?
- Showcase the three stages for a company to self-assess – are you working at a best-in-class, best practices, or standard operating procedures level right now?

Figuratively move your customers off the plant floor/out of their offices, and help them see where the world is going. Whenever these learning moments happen for me (such as recently understanding our CAGR benchmark) it's exhilarating. (Albeit frustrating at the same time, because you wonder why it took you so long to understand the topic.)

Chapter 11: Sales Play 4 – What does the Emerald City look like?

"Tell me and I forget, teach me and I may remember, involve me and I learn."

– Benjamin Franklin

This play is one of my favorites. I'd like you to remember the movie *The Wizard of Oz*, in which Dorothy and her motley crew of friends (Scarecrow, Tin Man, and Lion) are trying to get to the land of Oz, to visit the wizard inside the Emerald City. Along their journey, they encounter some pretty hairy situations, like fighting trees and flying attack monkeys... and understandably they get pretty discouraged. What I believe would have motivated and better guided this team is a clear picture of what the Emerald City looks like, what it smells like, and what its benefits are. Given this information in advance, Dorothy would have been more determined to keep marching on to the Land of Oz.

Using my silly analogy, I want you to picture your engagement strategy. Your prospective customers are more willing to shift priorities and change *if* they can gain a clear roadmap of what "better" looks like. They also need to be able to figuratively touch it, smell it, and taste it. This is what makes experiential marketing so effective. As a sales professional, your customer might not be able to literally "touch" your solution (unless you're able to develop a mock environment for them to use – a great way to execute this play), so here are ideas from our customers:

- Take a page out of the real estate industry. When you buy a home, you can now do virtual walkthroughs of the property. From the comfort of your living room, you can virtually walk from room to room and check out the neighborhood on Google Earth. You can literally imagine yourself living in that home, cooking, having friends over, etc. This same process is possible in all sales ecosystems now. Our customers have designed virtual CX experiences for their world, and made "day in a life" videos. A prospective customer can see themselves in this "day in a life". Think of a way to get your customers daydreaming.

- Take the digital world into the experiential/live world. Some of our customers have decided that producing a digital CX experience is too costly/time prohibitive/disengaging, and chosen live meetings as their call-to-action instead. Customers of ours like Rockwell Automation will use rich media and digital sales activities to bring customers to live events for collaboration. They realize that if they invite the right people to collaborate, their "Emerald City" happens with peer-to-peer collaboration.

What does the Emerald City look like in your world? How can your prospective customers gain an experiential sneak peek behind the curtains to meet the wizard?

Chapter 12: Sales Play 5 – Role/Function Career Guidance

"We rise by lifting others."
Robert Ingersoll

Let me tell you a story. I was keynoting a sales event for General Electric in Shanghai, China, and had dinner with the executive team that evening. I sat next to the CMO of a GE division and asked her: "Can you think of a great sales professional you've met in your life?" She told me a story about a sales professional for HPE in Singapore who ran the following sales play:

> **Touch-point 1:** he invited her to a marketing event in Hong Kong that he recommended as a "need-to-go-to" event;
>
> **Touch-point 2:** following that event, he built her a roadmap of three other marketing events in China that she should attend in order to further her marketing acumen;

Touch-point 3: he continued to follow up on her progress after each event and her key learnings.

This CMO said that if she needs a solution that HPE offers, this sales professional in Singapore is the first call she'll make!

The goal here is to recognize that your customers have **people** who work within these organizations. These people, just like you, are seeking career advice, help, networks, etc.

Consider how you can:
- Broker introductions
- Let them know about new job opportunities
- Give them invitations to events they may otherwise not have had access to
- Provide them with data that would benefit them personally in their careers (such as renegotiating their compensation)

In short, how can you help the person – not just the company?

PART 3: ENGAGE your accounts with your prescriptive sales plays

Chapter 13: Time management – your account segmentation mindset

"Either you run the day or the day runs you."
– Jim Rohn

Why would we be talking about account segmentation before we start engaging customers? We haven't created any opportunities yet! This is a common mistake for sales professionals and sales organizations – they have no plan for what happens after a buyer shows interest/intent. Look at your own sales process today, and I'll bet that it resembles something like the following:

- Touch 50 leads today
- Call each of your accounts every two weeks
- Have 12 sales conversations per day
- Visit each of your accounts once a month

These are simplistic examples of models that belong in the 20th century. They lack a base in the realities of modern, digital technology that helps sales professionals understand:

- Which accounts, and key stakeholders within an account, have high propensity to buy?
- Which accounts, and key stakeholders within an account, are showing buying intent?
- Which other potential stakeholders in an account are demonstrating their involvement in the buying committee, through content consumption?

All the digital technology necessary to better segment accounts into logical focus groups is available. There is absolutely no need to call up and down a list, or give an equal amount of attention to each of your accounts, just because they are "on your named account list".

That's actually counter-productive. As an example, a Fortune 50 customer of ours had a revelation that each account in a sales professionals' Activation List WAS NOT CREATED EQUAL. Yet, their pre-designed sales process required a sales professional to touch all accounts an equal number of times. In fact, the Buying Pyramid, created by Chet Holmes, indicates that approximately 10% of customers are really seeking change at any given moment. With that basic premise, our customer used artificial intelligence to review multiple historical data sets on their leads, and machine learning to further enhance their future "propensity to buy" lead recommendations.

The finding was shocking, but also game changing for their business – they discovered a Pareto's Law of lead value. Essentially, 20% of their leads created more than 80% of the closed-won opportunities in their business. Their next step shocked their thousands of sales professionals: they reduced the required number of accounts per sales professional by 80%! Think of the guts it took for those sales leaders to explain to the board of directors what they were doing. In their minds, this wasn't a risk but a simple calculation of time, energy, and results. They had all the propensity scoring models they needed. In combining this new account-focused "propensity scoring" system with digital selling activities, the average sales professional **doubled** their lead conversion, while continuing to grow lead volumes, in just 90 days! The key was a customer-centric focus combined with a digital sales approach.

Create your own "If This, Then That" Activation Cycle
As a sales professional, the only thing you can truly control is your own activity. Your activities are meant to highly influence sales objectives such as lead requirements, pipeline coverage requirements, and closed-won deals. Within your activities, you have three levers that help you understand where to adjust your activities:

a. **Volume:** How many accounts should I have in an Activation Cycle at all times? How many should I have activated and turned into opportunities? On average, how many sales plays will be required to activate an account?

b. **Velocity**: How long should my Activation Cycle be, before I run or replace an account? How often should I be replacing disengaged/lost accounts with new accounts? What should my sales play cadence/sequence be? How long should I wait between sales plays before disengaging accounts?

c. **Probability:** How much energy should I spend on my named accounts (longer sales cycles, but larger returns) vs. my Sphere of Influence accounts? How are specific Sphere of Influence accounts better engaging, and what are their commonalities? How probable is it for specific accounts to re-engage me after going dark for multiple months?

Step 1: Create categories to use for segmenting the accounts in your Activation List
For simplicity, I highly recommend you use basic categories, such as:

- Seeking to Activate
- Activated
- Replace

Seeking to Activate: The start position of all accounts in your Activation List. You have either not attempted to activate yet (you're just starting your sales play cycle), have no engagement, or have some level of engagement, but nothing that qualifies as buying intent. Essentially, the data on this account is inconclusive at the moment.
Activated: You have achieved a sufficient level of buying intent. Every sales environment is different, but you've most likely had sales conversations of some capacity. An example would be where a discovery call has been scheduled, and a next step has been secured.
Replace: You have no engagement and/or buying intent. At the cycle completion of sales plays for that account, you remove this account from your Activation List and identify a new account to add.

Step 2: Select the number of sales plays to deploy in an Activation Cycle
In Part 2 we outlined five example sales plays. That doesn't mean you should necessarily have five – you might want seven, or ten.

Depending on your customer's average sales cycle timeline, you can have as many sales plays in your cycle as you like. The goal here is to define and select your own ideal number of sales plays for one Activation Cycle, and execute that plan. Do not deviate from this plan! That's called "random acts of selling". This is a common fail for account-based programs. Some of our customers originally talked about "maybe we should have… I don't know, say… five sales plays?", but then left the design and execution of sales plays at the discretion of the sales professional. Others expect that marketing will design all the sales plays. Again, you're back to random acts of selling, where sales professional A replaces accounts after three sales plays, sales professional B has only one sales play, and sales professional C uses five sales plays. Operating in this way you have no idea where the chink in your armor might be. When you design sales plays, you should build an Activation Cycle and execute on that plan!

Step 3: Select a length of time for your Activation Cycle, and the cadence/sequence between sales plays

Determining the velocity of a completed Activation Cycle is best conducted by reverse-engineering your typical sales cycle timelines, while keeping in mind how to best influence your sales objectives. What you're trying to achieve here is deploying highly valuable information to a customer in a short enough time horizon that it potentially reduces your average sales cycles, and/or increases your win conversions. Executing a strong account-based motion is counter-intuitive if you end up winning new targeted accounts, only to have doubled your average sales cycle. Unless your LTV ends up three times larger, you may have just broken even from a cash flow perspective.

In the +300 customers we've worked with, the typical Activation Cycle will run for 30 to 90 days (for non-Enterprise accounts), before an account is transferred to Activated (see Part 4) or Replaced. Don't necessarily take the obvious route of dividing your natural sales cycle timeline equally by the number of sales plays you developed. For example, it's too simplistic to say: "I'm going to design my Activation Cycle over a 90-day time horizon, and I have six sales plays I've designed, so I must execute these plays every two weeks". In fact, we typically see that it's favorable for companies to front-load their sales play cadence. The rationale is time management – if you can complete your Activation Cycle quickly, you can also more quickly qualify accounts into Run or

Replace categories. As a sales leader, I would hate to see you spin your wheels with the same accounts for a quarter, only to attend the next quarterly business review (QBR) with a pipeline coverage report filled with inactivated accounts. It's better to fail fast and move onto new accounts.

Step 4: Select the time allocated for each touch-point within each a sales play, and the total number of touch-points within that single sales play
Remember that, within a sales play, you may have a series of touch-points. A common example of this is a sales play centered around a virtual or live event. The touch-points required may have a series of associated activities such as phone calls, emails, mailers, social engagement, etc. to attract the customer's attention to the event. Your touch-points may also be a burst of energy around one sales play (phone, email, LinkedIn connection, direct Twitter message) all in 24 hours, or you may have the sales play executable over the course of one week.

Step 5: IF account is activated, THEN connect account to a learning path
Once an account is activated, there will be a learning path, which we'll cover in Part 4. If an account is not activated during the Activation Cycle, there needs to be a Service Level Agreement (SLA) between marketing, sales leadership and the sales professional on the **objective** next step for that account. Unfortunately, sales professionals commit the deadly sin of emotional attachment every day: they want the account so bad (for brand recognition, potential revenue and commissions, or for personal reasons) that they can't see when they should step away. We'll talk more about objective vs. emotional attachment to accounts in Part 5.

Best-in-class teams have defined criteria for the continuance or removal (Run or Replace) of an account after it's completed an Activation Cycle, as it may adversely affect a sales professional's sales pipeline coverage. This does not mean, however, that these companies are abandoning all Account-based Marketing (ABM) efforts on that account. In fact, this is where ABM really takes the account back under its wings, for future activation. What also happens for many of our customers is that an account removed from the sales professionals hands and given to marketing is not necessarily placed in an ABM motion, but placed in an open-account marketing motion. The account and contacts transition into a "general pool" of leads that will be nurtured with blogs, infographics, webinars, etc. What isn't happening is that sales and marketing fall in love with that account (one that's clearly demonstrating a "cardiac arrest" propensity to buy), and marketing isn't desperately trying to create a glimmer of a heartbeat by spending more time, money and energy attempting to shock it into action.

Chapter 14: Digital selling within your sales plays

"If an opportunity doesn't knock, build a door."
– Milton Berle

The modern, digital sales professional has incredible tools at their disposal to accelerate their account-based motion. Never in sales history have the opportunities been so bright. Yet never in sales history have companies flamed out so much by drowning in tool fatigue, poor usage and adoption, and hyper-inflated cost-of-customer acquisition (CAC) from SaaS (Software-as-a-Service) application fees. In 2016, when *Social Selling Mastery®* was released, sales acceleration, sales performance and social sales tools were in their "early-adoption" phase. Globally these tools are still in their early days, but their widespread adoption has created a divergence of sales problems. Specifically, the poor usage and adoption, compounded with required ROI data for CFOs to justify these accelerated expenses. This has placed enormous pressure on sales leaders. We at Sales for Life use multiple tools as an ACCELERANT to our already structured sales process and skillsets. Before your sales organization begins to invest in tools for your account-based motion, please remember the fundamentals:

Change the mindset, then improve the skillset, and finally invest in the toolkit.

1. **Change the mindset**: You have to be fully committed to an account-based motion that has the proper internal acceptance, plan and execution strategy. Tools like LinkedIn Sales Navigator do an excellent job in helping you unlock data on Sphere of Influence accounts, but their value is really limited if you didn't understand the reason *why* you'd focus on high social proximity and asymmetrical competitive advantages. Furthermore, if you're unwilling to plan your storyboards and create truly customer-centric sales

plays, then the skills required for your customer engagement will be limited to basic tools like phone call scripts, email templates and social messages that will probably fall on deaf ears. You have to be willing to think in a bold and different way to gain your customers' attention.

2. **Improve the skillset:** I have heard this line maybe 100 times on discovery calls: "We want to do Social Selling training, because we have poor social platform adoption like LinkedIn, Twitter, Xing, WhatsApp and WeChat". It's great that you can see a skill gap, but what is the root cause, and what is the key driver to increase platform proficiency? You need to link your solution to a business outcome. Real business outcomes look like the following:

   - Increase sales quota attainment from 50% to 80% by increasing new logo acquisition per sales professional;
   - Upsell/cross-sell our key customers by 20%;
   - Create five new channel partnerships that yield 10 new accounts each in the next fiscal year.

   These are business outcomes, nothing to do with platform proficiency. Veiled behind companies looking for greater LinkedIn Sales Navigator adoption is a swath of Sales Enablement/Sales Operations teams simply seeking to justify their expenditure, not necessarily aligning towards a business outcome. That's why "skillset" comes after mindset. You have to start with a mindset to design, execute and hold sales professionals accountable to sales plays that highly influence sales objectives, which ultimately align to business outcomes. Be process-centric first, then you'll recognize the competencies that are required to achieve the sales goal. An investment in skills is ALWAYS a less expensive and more effective path to sales growth (measured by ROI and scale) than a tool or hiring more people will ever be. Yielding 5%, 10% or 20%

more throughput per sales professional may only cost you \$1,000 to \$2,500 per sales professional (remember that tools don't skill themselves up and execute themselves, people obtain skills to work with the tools), but it's worth it if a single sales professional can return you an incremental \$100,000 to \$1,000,000 in ROI with that small skills investment.

3. **Invest in the toolkit: Your account-based toolkit MUST be an accelerant to an existing motion, not the motion itself.** This can include marketing automation platforms, sales acceleration tools, data intelligence and/or social platforms. The tool is not the strategy! The tool is the means by which the strategy is better executed. At the time of writing, there are dozens of account-based marketing (ABM) tools available. We could fill a book just with tool analysis, but we'll leave tool selection up to you.

Account-based toolkit for the modern, digital sales professional

Remember what you're trying to accomplish in your sales engagement:

> **Priority 1:** Can I activate this account = YES OR NO?
> **Priority 2:** How can I leverage triggers, insights, referrals and competitive intelligence within my sales plays to best accomplish activating accounts? Simple.

> Before we outline the toolkit that you'll want to develop, let me present you with an example, at a sales leadership level, of a grave error that I see countless companies make (and I mean I've seen it hundreds of times). Without fail, each week we at Sales for Life receive a call or email from a company somewhere in the world that falls in one of these categories:
> 1. We recently purchased LinkedIn Sales Navigator, and are asking ourselves "now what?"

2. We're halfway through our LinkedIn Sales Navigator annual subscription and looking at the usage reports asking ourselves "really, are you serious??"
3. We're approaching our LinkedIn Sales Navigator annual renewal date, and the CFO has just asked the sales leadership team to "build me a business case for retaining these licenses, because I don't see it".

It's frustrating because we know how immensely effective LinkedIn Sales Navigator can be.

LinkedIn Sales Navigator is like driving a Porsche

As you'll have seen by now, I love analogies – so humor me with another here.

Your sales professionals are like daily commuters: they need to get from point A to point B each day, as quickly and efficiently as possible. While every commuter may choose their own unique path for getting to point B, each commuter will absolutely confirm that getting there more quickly is really important.

You decide to license each commuter a car for one year. And not just any car: a top-range Porsche 911 each. You smile and think to yourself: "Check the box, I've solved the problem of our commuters being late!" However, as the weeks go by you find out that many of the Porsches have never left the garage, and many of the commuters are still taking their previous mode of transportation. What? How is this possible? You even had them watching videos of Porsche's new "defensive driving" module, and had them read the user manual to help them learn to drive. Welcome to Pareto's Law, which states that 80% of the impact comes from 20% of the people. To continue with the car analogy, here's how Pareto's Law is applied here:

- 20% of the Porsches are being used daily, and they have helped commuters shave 30 minutes off their daily travel time;
- 60% of the Porsches are used sparingly, as it turns out that 50% of the those commuters have never

driven a manual transmission car, so they are struggling and frustrated with their daily commute. They're often heard saying "forget this, I'll stick to what I know";

- 20% of the Porsches have never left the garage because you forgot one critical point: 20% of the commuters don't have a driver's license!

Whatever stage you're in, don't for a minute believe that buying Porsche 911s (aka. LinkedIn Sales Navigator licenses) will solve your problem. Fast cars can be tools for commuting more quickly, but only race car drivers can turn hot laps around the track. Likewise, LinkedIn Sales Navigator is a tool, and you can ill afford a massive skill gap or discrepancy of usage when you approach your annual renewal, as any CFO will question this purchase.

Step 1: Competency benchmarking
Find out where your sales professionals sit in their digital readiness. Create a comparison with competitors and best-in-class. Don't live in a bubble. And certainly don't think a few videos will turn your sales professionals into race car drivers.

Step 2: Overcome the "WHY"
Don't assume your sales professionals automatically understand why digital tools are leveraged to select, plan, engage, activate and run accounts. Push each sales professional off their status quo to change today, not tomorrow. Remember, some of your commuters actually think the subway is a better mode of transportation than a Porsche. You have to build a business case for your Porsche 911 investment, even if it seems so obvious to you.

Step 3: Execute the "HOW"
Race car drivers are not going to take driving advice from a mechanic that's never driven a car before. Do not expect your social media marketing manager to drive sales results effectively for your sales team – there just won't be the level of upfront respect necessary to drive change. Only those that have "carried a bag" can teach those that "carry a bag."

Step 4: Reinforce the "WHAT"

Put in the hours to create change, as this is a habit no different than driving. "One and done" is a recipe for 10% retention rates. Think along the lines of Malcolm Gladwell's book *Outliers*, which suggests that it takes 10,000 hours to master a skill – it's unlikely that a two-hour workshop will be a solution. When you were learning to drive in your teenage years, how much time did your parents and driving instructor spend showing you how to drive a junk box car, let alone a Porsche? Don't start blowing up your accounts without the proper skills for engagement.

Account-based tool categories

There are five sales tool categories that you'll want to evaluate to best prepare yourself. In this section we're just highlighting a **few** tools that have become standard operating procedures for many of our customers, but many industry or situational tools will be great complements.

Tool Categories:
- Selection
- Insights
- Engagement
- Segmentation
- Learning Paths

Tools for Account Selection:

Goals:

i. to save time selecting accounts (such as Sphere of Influence accounts) that yield greater probability/conversion and faster velocity to activation.

ii. for named accounts, the ability to digitally surround key stakeholders, the buying committee, and the industry influencers.

The best global tool for this is LinkedIn Sales Navigator (see showcase later in chapter). If LinkedIn doesn't present you with valuable customer data (specific geographic markets, or verticals that have low adoption at the time of the writing of this book), you'll have to find other predictive tools that help with "high social proximity" and/or "propensity scoring". At IBM in LATAM, they have an internal cognitive sales advisory tool that feeds from Watson. Remember, you're **not** looking for account lists – you can find that basic data from a Google search. You're looking for asymmetrical competitive advantages that your competitors can't access because of your customer success, relationship, and/or customer engagements.

Tools for Account Insights:
Goal: to increase the speed and volume of contact identification, contact/account mapping for social proximity, and internal/external triggers that may lead to a higher probability for activation. Think about the micro and macro insights for:

    i. Key stakeholders
   ii. Key stakeholder relationships
  iii. Competitive intelligence
  iv. Industry/market trends

Social media platforms like LinkedIn, Twitter and Facebook have become key. The ultimate internet crawlers for data are Google Alerts and Google Trends. Some of our customers have used industry/data specific tools such as:

- Form 10-K (public companies are listed, but used for industry, market and competitive intelligence)
- Owler
- Glassdoor
- Alexa
- Job boards like Indeed.com (role hiring, departmental growth, account growth trends)
- Conducting your own market, industry or company intelligence with free Google Survey

Tools for Account Engagement:
Goal: to increase the probability of account activation through a more personal and educationally rich digital experience.
- LinkedIn PointDrive (see showcase later in chapter)
- Vidyard GoVideo (see showcase later in chapter)
- Cadence/Sequence tools such as Salesloft, Outreach.io

Tools for Account Segmentation:
Goal: to focus your energy on specific accounts, and increase the probability of activating those accounts showing proper buying intent. These engagement tools can showcase buying intent and buyer committee mapping data.
- LinkedIn PointDrive
- Vidyard GoVideo
- Cadence/Sequence tools such as Salesloft, Outreach.io

Tools for Learning Paths:
Goal: to increase the probability of account wins by overcoming key questions, obstacles and pitfalls, while reducing sales cycle timelines in the process. Providing a rich-media library of content that will push a buyer off their status quo, and allow the sales team to monitor the content consumption story of their buyers.
- LinkedIn PointDrive
- Clearslide
- Postwire
- EveryoneSocial, LinkedIn Elevate, or Feed.ly

For content aggregation (collecting content from around the internet), we like to use both EveryoneSocial and Feed.ly. While Feed.ly is great for flagging blogs and news articles on any topic around the world, EveryoneSocial is centralized into our marketing automation and CRM, allowing us to see which sales professional shared which content, to drive which customer engagement. This allows us to measure content at a granular level and see the "content consumption story" of an account. The tool also allows us to organize both curated and internally created content. We organize the content in a sales-centric manner (by buyer persona, buyer journey stage, asset type, etc.) so that we can find the appropriate insights quickly and share with our accounts.

Deep dive into our favorite tools (at the time of writing):

LinkedIn PointDrive

The tool itself will be unique to your customer experience, but it's HOW you leverage PointDrive that provides the real value. LinkedIn PointDrive is free for any Navigator user – if you haven't been getting enough from Navigator to justify the investment, this could be the deciding factor. Picture a landing page, but one that's a blank canvas. On each landing page, you have the ability to share complex ideas, best practices, pitfalls, challenges, implementation road maps, proposals, contracts, pricing scenarios... the possibilities are endless.

Creative sales professionals realize that sharing a PowerPoint presentation with customers does nothing to better serve the customer experience. PointDrive is rich media that can be passed from key stakeholder to stakeholder in an account.

Now here is where your time management becomes critical. Each person in an account that opens your PointDrive landing page is now tracked, giving you their LinkedIn information, how long they spend on the page, what pages/videos they viewed, etc. Forget the marketing automation data other companies have; you, the sales professional, have complete insight into your customers' buying intent and engagement.

Use Case 1: LDR/SDR/BDR – lead segmentation on touch-point 1

You have a basket of leads (inbound or outbound). You might have preliminary *buying intent* information from marketing automation or other sources, but how do you really focus your time? You can use this tool to segment accounts into three categories: *hot, warm or cold*, based on the lead's engagement (even those that marketing has passed over as a "hot lead"). You will deploy sales plays (using LinkedIn PointDrive) to each lead, and monitor their engagement. This is a major time-saver. You gain a clear picture of how strong this lead is. Customers of ours have doubled their lead conversion by spending way, way, way more effort on "the new hot leads", and reducing effort for the warm and cold. The data doesn't lie... it's best to spend a lot of time on the hot leads, then balance your efforts on the other leads.

Use Case 2: Account Executive – lead/account qualification
Best-in-class companies will develop sales plays based on implementation successes, case studies, pitfalls/challenges to avoid, etc. so that you can tailor these sales plays to each account (and the buying committee within the accounts), to get a sense of buying intent. Thus, you aren't just measuring "is this account interested?", you're also measuring "what topics are they interested in?" You can capture insights on each idea as you present them in various formats: video, PDF, PowerPoint, blog form, etc., and now you can focus on their interests.

Use Case 3: Account Executive – building consensus in the buying committee (and discovering new players)
The death of deals can happen when new players appear at the 11th hour and completely disrupt the flow. In that situation, wouldn't you want to know who the mystery buying committee members might be? You are now using LinkedIn PointDrive to share critical information with your customers to help align the buying committee. Each time a buying committee member forwards this information onto their teammates in order to build internal consensus, you're notified of who that person is.

500 million people have a LinkedIn account, so rest assured you'll capture valuable information. If a particular buying committee member is not on LinkedIn, they still need to fill in a quick form to access the materials.

Use Case 4: Account Executive – shortening the velocity of the deal (proposal-to-close)
A global software customer of ours used PointDrive to design a variety of FAQ pages, answering the top five implementation questions a customer typically asks before they buy. Whenever our customer sends a proposal or contract, they also send FAQ-based PointDrives to the customer. Within 90 days, data started appearing in their CRM showing that they had reduced their average time from proposal-to-close by 14 days. Customers didn't need to tie up expensive solution consultants' time to answer their final questions (which could take time going back and forth in scheduling a call), they had their questions addressed in the LinkedIn PointDrive. At scale, that's massive from a cash flow perspective!

Use Case 5: Customer success – reduce churn or upsell/cross-sell
This tool is exceptionally powerful for educating customers, introducing new ideas, use cases, best practices, etc. You can deploy new ideas to your accounts, measure interest levels, gauge topics of interest, and align buying committees in new divisions that you may not have been aware of. As an example, one of the top sales professionals inside Microsoft's LATAM offices in Costa Rica builds a weekly newsletter for her top 100 accounts. You own the account, and this tool is both an educator and a time management machine.

Vidyard GoVideo
Vidyard GoVideo is a video creation and sharing platform that hosts your videos in the Cloud. Each video has a unique hyperlink that you can share using any digital communication platform, such as email or social. Much like LinkedIn, the value creation is less about the uniqueness of the tool, and more about the value you bring in your message. But is video messaging really effective? And if so, how effective is it? Our sales team has been using video messaging for approximately two years, and we've empirically proven that it engages customers with a higher conversion rate than traditional communication methods like phone and email. As an example, here is a test I conducted in April 2017:

I Tested Which InMails Got the Best Response Rates—Here Are the Results

Each test message group received 300 LinkedIn InMails to the same Buyer Persona, Industry & Geography

Test Message A: The text-based HARD selling call-to-action
Results: 5.5% response rate, $0 sales in 30 days from campaign

My message style was very simple a direct:
    a. Question to push the buyer off their status quo
    b. Statement with empirical data to solve perceived challenge
    c. Landing page link
    d. CTA to schedule a call

I didn't have a lot of faith in this messaging style, and the data was pretty clear. Most of the 5.5% responses were a HARD NO, as I didn't build any value. Some respondents were actually angry at me for being a product pusher!

Test Message B: The text-based open-ended discussion starter
Results: 11.5% response rate, $12,000 sales in 30 days from campaign.

This open discussion was meant to gauge two interests:
- a. Has the topic of Social Selling been a key priority to your business?
- b. IF YES, has our content been a core staple to your personal development?

The follow-up discussions had two paths, each based on the buyer's interest in Social Selling and personal development. Think of the message as a filtration process. The messaging style clearly showed me that LinkedIn InMails can be used similar to Facebook, Google or Twitter chats. Remember most buyers read and respond via mobile, where the InMail conversation thread is very chat-like. Those that moved further into the sales process (and purchased) needed to have immediate, definitive interest in Social Selling – specifically as this campaign was for only 30 days. That doesn't mean others that I had discussions with won't become buyers in the future... they will!

Test Message C: The text-based highly personalized discussion + HARD Selling call-to-action

Results: 17.5% response rate, $12,000 sales in 30 days from campaign

These text-based messages were written specifically for each account. I leveraged Triggers, Insights or Referrals that were very, very specific to the key stakeholder personally, or their company.

    a. Major internal (such as Job Changes) or external (such as Merger & Acquisition activity) to contextualize the urgency to speak.
    b. Relationship "Sphere of Influence" connection to our customer base.
    c. Insights from their competitors showing a shift in the market, and the risk vs. opportunity.

Context really helped here. Buyers can clearly tell when I'm focusing my message directly at them.

Test Message D: The video-based 1-to-1 direct video message that's highly personalized, and includes a HARD-Selling call-to-action

Results: 37.3% response rate, $27,000 sales in 30 days from campaign

I'm going to let the data speak for itself! I make highly humanized, highly contextualized videos in a 1-to-1 relationship with the buyer. It's like I'm in the office sitting next to the buyer. What you can say in 60 seconds to synthesize all the best practices you've learnt, and then articulate that information to buyers, is much more powerful than a text-based email.

Chapter 15: Best-in-class sales plays in action

"There is a way to do it better – find it."
Thomas Edison

We've seen dozens and dozens of sales plays over the years. The plays that I most admire are the ones that are simple and easy to refine/repeatable, and that push customers to think in bold and different ways. There's a great clip on YouTube from an interview with Grant Cardone and Jarrod Glandt from Cardone Enterprises, where they talk about their internal four-step sales process. In the middle of the clip, Jarrod speaks up and says "when something isn't working, we (Cardone Enterprises) tend to not add a new process, but remove something. We simplify it." I think this is really important, because the most effective sales plays are not over-engineered marketing wonders, but simple-to-execute plays that get to the heart of a customer's problems. I've pulled together three example sales plays for you, and we'll outline why our customers found these plays so effective in engaging and activating their buyers.

SALES PLAY 1: Existing customer advocates refer new accounts with highly predictable results
Customer referrals are the holy grail of sales leads. Everyone knows that. Unfortunately, few sales professionals know HOW to mechanize the process even once, let alone in a predictable manner. This play is effective because each stage of the referral process is pre-designed into templates, and the sales play is repeatable for any sales professional. In addition, the templates are also made for the customer advocate to give to their referral, making the referral process frictionless at their end.

Step 1: Map your advocate's "Sphere of Influence"
Everyone has a Sphere of Influence, with specific people in their social network with high social proximity. Your customer advocates have a social proximity of at least two, three or four companies that they can introduce you to quickly, thereby shortening deal cycles by weeks or months. Use LinkedIn Sales Navigator to find these high social proximity accounts/contacts.

EXPERT TIP: Think about the **power of three**. Focus on either three people at one company, or three people at three companies – no more than this. Find three key stakeholders that match your buyer persona and that your advocate is clearly well connected to (social proximity is high).

Step 2: Design the introduction sales play

I once heard Barbara Giamanco say: "For every 20 referrals I ask for:

- 10 make an effort to place the introduction;
- 5 return a message;
- 2 turn into a meeting."

I might be paraphrasing here, but ultimately this is a numbers game. To dramatically increase your conversion rates, *do not* do the following:

Say, "Hi John, do you mind introducing me to three vice-presidents of sales in your network?" Guess what? John will probably have no idea where to start.

Instead, paint by numbers for John. Build a template that allows John to broker the introduction:

a. Explicitly outline the three people (maximum) you'd like an introduction to.

b. Give John the sales play he'll use, making it brain-dead simple.

Suggested referral message

John,
I hope you're doing well.

It's my pleasure to introduce you to Jamie Shanks, CEO at Sales for Life. Sales for Life is an excellent training & advisory resource for our business in helping us develop a leading social selling/digital selling program. They've built programs for hundreds of global companies, and I recommend your team talks to them about best practices.

Here is some quick information from Jamie: https://ptdrv.linkedin.com/xlptqp5

I'll leave it to you both to connect, and best of luck in your conversations.
Cheers,
  Bob Martin

EXPERT TIP: Leverage rich media (I like to use LinkedIn PointDrive) within your introduction. This way, the introduced new referral has much more context on you and your business.

SALES PLAY 2: Drive key stakeholders in an account to a live, experiential networking event

Several of our customers, including Rockwell Automation, Teleperformance, and Selligent Marketing Cloud, have recognized that opportunities happen when they can get their customers in live "collision points" with each other. The first buying sign is getting the customer out of the bubble of their office, and then creating peer-to-peer events for customers to meet, learn, and have intimate conversations. For some of these customers, they have an 80% win-rate when they can move a customer to a live event. These events can be one time (conferences), roadshows (multiples), or special/highly experiential (e.g., sporting events).

Step 1: Brainstorm the ultimate outcome for a live event

For some of our customers, the ultimate outcome is one-on-one face time. For others, it's placing a prospective customer at a table with existing customers and letting the peer-to-peer conversations do the selling for you. As a sales organization, reverse-engineer the outcomes you desire to find the actions and stories necessary to achieve those outcomes.

Step 2: Develop a compelling reason to meet live

What doesn't work (as well), is ad-hoc approaches to customers, like "I'm in your city, are you free next Tuesday?" You might gain a few quick meetings, but it's not a truly compelling reason for a customer to alter their breakfast, lunch, or – most importantly – evening plans away from family. You have to tell a story that paints the picture of value, opportunity cost of missing, and limited availability. People love feeling special that they're being invited to something that is exclusive.

Step 3: Build media-rich stories that drive interest

Customers need to see it, feel it, and visualize themselves at the event. Images and videos of the peers they'll meet, the speakers they'll learn from, the innovative products they'll gain exclusive first access to. Our customers that create multi-city roadshows will show video examples of the other city events.

SALES PLAY 3: "Massage their ego" with influencer blog articles and Top 10 lists

As an industry influencer, this sales play has been run on myself and Sales for Life a number of times. I can tell you that we now use the software from some of the companies that ran this sales play. The concept is really simple, but effective. You aim to gain the attention of key stakeholders in an account by publicly highlighting their accomplishments, which gains their attention, allowing you to create a relationship footprint in the account. The companies that have run highly effective versions of this play will craft content about these key stakeholders that aren't "fluff pieces", but really insightful assets that an industry would find valuable. Version 1.0 of this concept would be a Top 10 list, but best practice is crafting an article that has interlaced value with key stakeholder accolades. We've leveraged this sales play for existing customers of ours, and I can personally tell you that it's helped us win further engagements with customers as it's strengthened our relationship.

> **Pro Tip:** Best-in-class sales organizations run this sales play with marketing in lock-step. Marketing typically helps research and write the content for sales to distribute socially.

> **Step 1:** Select an account and map the key stakeholders.
> **Step 2:** Find a story that intertwines your core value proposition with great customer examples, and find ways to add your new account/key stakeholders into the story.
> **Step 3:** Share with and tag both the new account/key stakeholders and the other industry leaders tagged on the blog article.

PART 4: ACTIVATE your engaged accounts with tailored learning paths

Chapter 16: Account segmentation: developing learning paths by buying intent

"A good system shortens the road to a goal."
Ralph Waldo Emerson

We have already used account segmentation at the beginning of an Activation Cycle, seeking to Activate (Run) or Non-Activate (Replace), but let's concentrate on accounts you have activated. These accounts will not necessarily follow the linear buyer's journey that a typical marketing team designs. The classic marketer will assume the account will logically flow something like this:

1. Awareness
2. Consideration
3. Decision

This is a model popularized from Hubspot. It's fair to assume that this is your desired state, but I'm more inclined to focus on the realities that were showcased in *The Challenger Customer* book, called the "spinning plate" theory. The spinning plate theory recognizes that although you're targeting accounts, you're really selling to an assortment of people. All of these champions, decision-makers and influencers are working on various initiatives, with varying degrees of knowledge about the problem or your solution. A marketing model that assumes linear nurture paths is thus assuming that everyone in the account is traveling at the same speed, with the same knowledge/competency – which is just not correct.

The spinning plate, in brief definition, is an analogy for buyers learning at the same speed. Imagine that each buying committee member within an account is spinning a plate on their fingers, yet each plate is spinning at a different speed. Some are comfortably on a finger like a basketball, while some are seconds from crashing to the floor. This analogy represents you, the sales professional, and your responsibility to keep all plates across the whole committee spinning comfortably on all fingers. This requires various sales strategies for different people. I recommend you think about this "spinning plate" theory as you design your learning paths for activated accounts.

Once you really grasp the idea that your accounts are just filled with a collection of people you hope to align for a common goal, then you'll design your activated account segments based on mindsets and problems, not buying milestones. We believe there are three fundamental mindsets and problematic inflection-points you need to overcome for individual buying committee members. We'll dive deep into these three categories in Chapters 17-19, but we'll take a moment to highlight them here:

> **The dead zone:** The uncomfortable silence you receive when a key stakeholder is disengaged with you. Remember that we've already activated these accounts, so there is some level of buying intent. Unfortunately, the key stakeholder went dark – perhaps after the discovery call, or after you sent over a proposal. They *said* they would call you back next week... but it's been six weeks! How are you going to revive this buyer from the dead?

> **The Yellow Brick Road:** At some point in the sales cycle, you get the suspicion that a particular key stakeholder on the buying committee just doesn't get it. However you've been outlining the solution just seems to field more confused questions, blank staring, silence, or downright pushback. How can you straighten out their path? How can you turn something that seems complex to them into more easily digestible bite-size chunks? How can you have the key stakeholder focus on one step at a time, rather than be scared of the cascading effects your solution may have in their business long-term? Lay down the Yellow Brick Road for this key stakeholder, brick by brick.

> **The mental pretzel:** I personally get frustrated with this key stakeholder mindset more than any other in our business. This is the key stakeholder that assumes because they've read a few blogs, skimmed today's *Wall Street Journal* and asked their friend Larry, they *think* they're a resident expert on the topic. They commoditize complexity. You're

frustrated by their perceived arrogance and simplification of your solution. How can you help them understand the cascading effects of "ready, fire, aim", without designing a bigger strategic plan? How can you help a line manager think like a CEO, rather than only about their micro-initiatives? This is the art of a trusted advisor, and not a sales representative.

Chapter 17: Learning path 1: The dead zone

"Not adding value is the same as taking it away."
Seth Godin

I'd like you to go into your inbox and find a really crappy email outreach from a sales professional. Once you find that email, search for that sales professional's name in your inbox archive. What you're most likely going to see is a series of email messages that ALL LOOK SIMILAR. Not only is the copy clearly a template, but the value and education that this sales professional brought to you was one sales play… over and over again. Now reframe your thinking to that of a key stakeholder at a Top 10 account you're trying to win. As an example, imagine you are the Chief Human Resources Officer of a global company. You have been dealing with a sales professional, talking about Time & Attendance software, and personally you like what you see. But life gets in the way. You're thinking about payroll, a wrongful dismissal in your Canadian office, the new sexual harassment e-learning program, the L&D team you're launching in EMEA, the recruiting backlog that your RVP Sales in Americas are screaming about… the list is endless. Amongst all those challenges, the Time & Attendance software sales professional is emailing and calling you once a week. The messages look like this:

> Voicemail: "Hi Mary, this is John at HR Super Software. I know you're busy, but I'm just checking in on our last conversation. Call me."

> Email: "Hi Mary, I hope you're doing well. As per our call last week, any feedback? Are you ready to talk next steps? I've talked to finance about a 10% discount if we lock this up by the end of this month."

Each week, John sends you a slight variance on this messaging… week after week after week. What John doesn't understand is that you've gone silent because of priorities, not because you're actually dead. He doesn't understand that his point-solution is priority #14 on your "key initiatives for FY 2019". I want to reiterate this point:

John doesn't realize what your priorities are in order of operations, and where in the queue his solution fits into your strategic plans.

The dead zone is just like the tasks that you personally write down on your phone or sheets of paper each day/week. The dead zone is directly correlated to a buyer's priority levels. Yes, on occasion it's due to timing issues like vacations, deaths in the family or aligning calendars with key stakeholders. But in my experience, when a buyer wants to solve a problem they want to solve it yesterday. It's your responsibility to identify what they need to solve yesterday, what they can solve today, and what they can push to solve later.

Step 1: Brainstorm on value-drivers that shift priorities
Most solutions are budgeted, funded and/or purchased because they solve a problem that's hindering a business outcome. Your solution is a deliverable for achieving that outcome. Outcomes that become priorities have to fall into one of these three categories:
  a. Make the company more money;
  b. Save the company more money;
  c. Mitigate the risk of the key stakeholder or company failing, and causing a cascading waterfall of future problems.

If you can't align your solution to one or more of these outcomes (and not every solution in the world can), then you're going to be relegated to priority #14. There is nothing wrong with that if you have the volumes and velocity of sales pipeline to recognize that the key stakeholder will just buy when they're ready (e-commerce or commoditized solutions perhaps). But for the rest of us, we have to help the key stakeholder connect problems to solutions, and help with priority realignment. How are you going to help the key stakeholder realize that you can solve one or more of these problems today?

Step 2: Design sales plays that address these value-drivers
There are two ways to tackle this step.
  • Create a learning path addressing each of these three value-drivers, hoping that one resonates;
  • Create a learning path for the value-driver only you are capable of solving.

Of course, if you're selling a money-making solution to a buyer than needs only to reduce operational expenses by 17%, then you have issues that are outside the scope of this book. In designing your new learning path, and the series of sales plays that will necessitate that path, begin by writing down questions that you continue to hear in discovery calls, building consensus calls, proposal calls. Where do people get stuck? Where do you hear your solution having success with existing customers? If you don't have those answers yourself, have lunch with someone in your customer success/account management team. Find out how customers realized they were making money, saving money, mitigating risks, based on their hundreds of customer conversations. How have customers achieved value ONLY AFTER they've become YOUR customer, and can only realize these gains with you? You might need to get granular in your planning for Left Brain vs. Right Brain buyers (this will help you design your other two learning paths).

> **Left Brain**: The analytical thinker, who is perhaps in the dead zone because they can't see the logic of how your solution connects linearly to other initiatives in their company. This key stakeholder is factual, with structured thinking. In this instance, we've created ROI calculators in spreadsheets for customers.
>
> **Right Brain:** The creative "big" thinker, who is perhaps in the dead zone because you've failed to win their heart, as you "feature-dumped" on the last call. The key stakeholder is emotional, and can't see how this will boost their career internally.

Step 3: Identify THAT buyer's value-driver BEFORE deploying a learning path

Stop, step back, and think. You've got some time, given that you're already in the dead zone. Go back to your notes or CRM, read the company's / competitor's / vertical comparable Forms 10-K, read Glassdoor reviews, reach out to connections on LinkedIn that have an inside track on that company. You must seek to find out (even if you don't understand) what that key stakeholder's priorities are.

Step 4: Focus relentlessly on helping them accomplish their value-driver

Center your story ONLY on solving that problem, and deploy a series of sales plays that create urgency. Here are a few ideas for you:

- Invite them to an event – not a basketball game, something where they can learn and meet their peers. Let their peers help guide the key stakeholder.
- Have a customer advocate actually reach out to the key stakeholder to "give their head a shake" and tell a story about how they solved a similar challenge by deciding to change today, not tomorrow.
- Make a series of videos of a real customer environment. Draw on the Emerald City concept, but go deeper. Show the customer the opportunity cost of what they're missing.
- Offer free value, such as training and consulting. We do something called "The Hour of Power" where we'll train a sales team on a topic for free (typically live at their office). This really helps the customer understand how to connect our solution to an outcome.

Where sales professionals fail in the dead zone is by treating this scenario with a shotgun approach: the key stakeholder hasn't just deprioritized your solution, sales professionals with alternative "mindshare" stealing solutions are in the mix as well. In reality, the key stakeholder is thinking about three core initiatives right now, and probably for the next quarter. You either can chisel your way into the mindshare of those priorities, or you can remain in the dead zone.

Chapter 18: Learning path 2: The Yellow Brick Road

> "Complexity is your enemy. Any fool can make something complicated. It is hard to keep things simple."
> Richard Branson

Imagine you're in a live meeting, or on a video conference call, and one of the key stakeholders seems lost. Their questions feel repetitive, or perhaps others have talked over this person as their questions appeared redundant in meetings. DO NOT discount this person. I've seen these people be influencers to my champion (my champion even being the economic decision-maker), only to find out that this influencer turned into a detractor because they couldn't see this project happening. These types of people appear daft – for some reason they just can't see how this connects to driving value for their business. They might also be fearful that this project is too disruptive, not connected to bigger initiatives, too time intensive, etc.

Right now their brain is scrambled eggs; what seems so simple to you seems so daunting to them. Be prepared, because these types of buyers can really put a wrench in your plans if you can't build them a bridge to clarity.

Step 1: Think Left Brain and sketch out a linear path of connections, integrations and milestones
If you find a key stakeholder stuck on complexity, put yourself into the mind of a left brain thinker. Perhaps you haven't laid out a clear path of the journey from point A to B to C, etc. Your conversations or presentations thus far might be strategic, high-level, value-laced masterpieces, but "the devil's in the detail". Time for you to get detailed!

> Grab a sheet of paper and think about how you can show linear steps, with dates and milestones. In

professional services, we call these process, deliverables and outcomes. Inside Social Selling Mastery®, there are six process steps, six core deliverables, and one core outcome (increased sales pipeline and revenue). You may find that the economic decision—maker who will finance this solution is a Right Brain thinker, but the directors and line managers who will be the daily users want Left Brain details.

Step 2: Visualize the connections, integrations and milestones
Transpose your field sketch into a presentation that can be communicated in ONE PAGE. Remember, your responsibility is to make the complex seem simple to communicate, plan and execute. You're also saying to your key stakeholder "don't worry, we've got this for you".

At the time of writing, we have a one-page "process roadmap". This allows us to leverage our one-page asset in a variety of communication mediums like LinkedIn PointDrive, video, email, virtual or live presentations. This roadmap is the start to the process, deliverables, and outcomes conversation, which is further supported with granular details within each process stage. Each stage has a logical order of operations, and can easily be articulated on how it connects and integrates to their ecosystem and go-to-market strategy. Use the K.I.S.S. method (keep it simple, stupid).

Step 3: Simplify everything down to focus on baby steps and/or how to get started
Your key stakeholder might be mentally three chess moves ahead, and can only see implications, pitfalls, further internal collaboration/committees… and pain, pain, pain for their role (an inability to see themselves managing this solution is often the reason why they become a detractor in the first place). If you've ever downhill skied before, I want you to stop for a second and remember your first experience. Think of how daunting it seemed.

- Equipment: where do I start?
- That mountain seems so huge!
- How do I navigate this lodge?
- How do I get on the chairlift?

- Do I snow plow, or do I slide side-to-side?
- How am I ever going to get off this mountain???

Downhill skiing has hundreds of factors: these sorts of daunting questions have many people quitting before they even get started. You must be the ski coach to your key stakeholder, and reassure them:

- The pain of doing nothing is more taxing and dangerous than something;
- I will be your coach;
- There is a coaching plan.

We have personally found that this key stakeholder archetype is most concerned about the value-driver of mitigating risk/failure. The risk of failure, looking foolish and being unable to execute may overwhelm their other value-drivers. For this type of key stakeholder, they will need to trust you first, then trust your process.

Chapter 19: Learning path 3: The mental pretzel

> "We cannot solve our problems with the same thinking we used when we created them."
> – Albert Einstein

I loathe encountering this buyer. This buyer is somehow in the luxurious position of being able to take complex solutions and make them seem so simple that they wonder why they just don't do it themselves (or why you don't provide it to them for free). Meet either the "know-it-all" or the "just check a box" key stakeholder. Either one of these key stakeholders can be very frustrating. How can you help them realize that simple isn't that simple? In our world, these are the sales and marketing leaders that say "LinkedIn is social selling, I've got some of that – I just bought LinkedIn Sales Navigator. We're good". That's like me saying "I know what Waste Management Corp. does – they're garbagemen. Pick up garbage, dump garbage… simple!" Clearly the board of directors of Waste Management would laugh me out of the room if I breezed over the logistics of storage, incineration, bio-fuels, recycling, energy trading, etc. that are part of their business. How can you help this key stakeholder realize the ramifications of short-sightedness or over-simplifying the ability to generate a massive outcome?

Step 1: Think Right Brain and sketch out outcomes, showing how each decision will affect those outcomes
This buyer can be both a blessing and a curse. They are often the big thinker, and might want to start yesterday. They aren't in the weeds of the project, thus they may not care how it works, they're only concerned with how you turn the light switch on to make an outcome appear. Their naivety brings forth:

- commoditizing your solution or pricing model (smaller project scopes, smaller LTV)
- poor implementation and eventually churn issues

You need to articulate that the "devil in the details, and it's those details that you're paying the big money for". We recommend you start sketching out ideas, moving from macro to micro:

- What is the overarching value-driver that this key stakeholder is trying to achieve?
- What are the core milestones, objectives and decision-making inflection points adversely affecting that value-driver or outcome that this key stakeholder will need to think about?
- What self-reflective questions can I get the key stakeholder asking themselves to re-address their own logic?

This is important. You're trying to get the key stakeholder to question themselves. The buyer has to be shown the opportunity cost of their over-simplified decisions.

Step 2: Visualize your decision-tree or category ecosystem
Turn your sketch into a visual representation of decisions and/or ecosystem thinking. The buyer has to see what their short-sighted or over-simplified thinking really looks like.
In our digital selling example, here is our current understanding of the digital selling ecosystem. This world is evolving every year. How can a buyer possibly assume that LinkedIn is digital selling after:

a. Reviewing the digital selling ecosystem
b. Sharing insights on each part of the ecosystem that helps the buyer benchmark their outcomes vs. best-in-class

Step 3: Get the key stakeholder talking to your customers
Speaking to customers works for all learning paths, but it's extra-valuable for this archetype. The key stakeholder needs to hear about the journey, the details, the internal friction, how they overcame obstacles, and ultimately how perseverance led to great outcomes. These battle scars are the details they might be breezing over. Your customers may also help with thinking bigger and more long-term, now that they have seen the benefits on the other side of implementation. We've leveraged our customers, like Microsoft,

when we're working with a global account that has a sales enablement leader that's thinking short-term, "checking a box" or thinking small. One phone call to Microsoft helps the key stakeholder realize that global scale with meaningful sales pipeline impact is not "purchase LinkedIn = your company is now Social Selling".

Chapter 20: Best-in-class learning paths in action

"The path of a sound credence is through the thick forest of skepticism."
George Jean Nathan

When you're designing your learning paths, don't assume that everything has to focus on digital platforms like LinkedIn or video. Not at all. In fact, the most successful learning paths that we've seen combine digital, analog and experiential as a hybrid-learning environment. As you're reading this book, you might say to yourself "wow, I can't do this!" Remember, I didn't write this book to give you sales plays on standard operating procedures that your competitors run on a daily basis. I'm showing you what the highest performing sales professionals are doing to dominate, and hope to inspire you to create your own ideas. Here are a few examples to get your creative juices flowing:

A weekly "digital newsletter" for the healthcare vertical in LATAM

As we deployed our Digital Selling Fundamentals course to all Microsoft inside sales centers globally, we met a fantastic sales professional in their Costa Rica office. She's also the number one sales professional, which won't surprise you after reading this best practice. She had been assigned 100 pharmaceutical and healthcare accounts to target, with the mission of helping these accounts understand the power of cloud computing (Microsoft Azure product). Each of her 100 accounts had already been activated, but the buyers and buying committees within those accounts were all at various stages in their cloud computing journey.

Recognizing that the Latin American Market (LATAM) was hungry for insights, she decided to become her own digital newsletter. She began by collecting stories, use cases and new innovations of cloud computing usage in hospitals from Mexico City to Lima to Bogotá to Buenos Aires. Every Friday, she compiles these stories into a newsletter that she creates inside a LinkedIn PointDrive. Once complete, she emails this newsletter to her buyers and the ever-growing buying committee of readers. The insights tab in LinkedIn PointDrive means she can see any new reader of her newsletter.

In February 2018, when I was in their office for training, she told me that she had recently been ill on a Friday and skipped the publication. On the Monday, she had a number of key stakeholders email her looking for the weekly newsletter, because their company was using it for updates on new innovation in LATAM. She now has 30% of her email database consume her insights on a weekly basis. She's become the trusted advisor to that market, and paves her "Yellow Brick Road" for her customers with a visually focused medium like LinkedIn PointDrive.

Experiential tours of work/solution environments

Don't just tell key stakeholders how a solution works, show them! In one example, Showpad and Minds & More (a sales consulting company in Brussels, Belgium) partnered to bring sales leaders together to learn from each other and decode/demystify what best-in-class sales organizations in Belgium were doing to succeed. This particular learning path was cool on wheels! They hired a bus holding 12-15 and gathered a group of VP Sales in a comfortable roundtable environment; in true Belgian style, the bus had beer taps and DJ on board. These VP Sales travelled together from technology company to technology company, experiencing innovative ideas to add to their sales process. These sales leaders were able to acquire more go-to-market knowledge in one afternoon than most would learn in one year. While this might not be the world's most scalable account-based learning path, the sales conversions are industry shattering. While the average opportunity-to-win rate for technology companies is 25%-30%, our customers have said that their offline experiential events can yield upwards of 80% conversion.

Create an industry-specific association in a geographic market

I like to consider myself a creative person, but when we saw this customer learning path, I was elated (and also sworn to secrecy on the details). Our customer had recognized that a specific vertical they were targeting was devoid of an industry accreditation and association. While this vertical had tradeshows and conferences like most others, there wasn't a certification process or association governing body that could elevate the vertical with best practices. So they stepped in.

To get started, the sales professional partnered with marketing to help with the initiative.

Together they wrote a business plan for the executive leadership to help fund this account-based plan. At that time, the company had a few successes in that vertical, but nothing that would scream "this is a great bet, we already own a majority market share in that vertical". This was definitely a learning experience. Next the sales professional and marketing team began to interview their existing customers in the vertical, and the analysts that support that industry. This helps our customer formulate events and association resources that are actually in high demand:

- A vertical group on social media (like LinkedIn for forum discussions) and live event chatter
- Association badges for the members on their LinkedIn profiles
- An annual conference that has analysts speaking at the event and helping the members

Our customer keeps the association at arm's length. They are visible in the association, but not overtly marketing to the group. This particular learning path is not for the impatient. From set-up to highly functional association can take years. This might be a sales play for your enterprise sales professionals. But the result is simple: they've choked out their competition from an entire vertical – literally. They own this market.

PART 5: RUN OR REPLACE your accounts

Chapter 21: Account objectivity over emotion

"What objectivity and the study of philosophy requires in not an 'open mind', but an active mind – a mind not just able and eagerly willing to examine ideas, but to examine them critically."
– Ayn Rand

I'll be the first to admit that I've become too attached to an account before. I can vividly remember being so emotionally invested in these deals that it's altered my mood at home. I'm a passionate sales professional, and I want every opportunity. I'm not one of those awful "zero-sum" entrepreneurs that wants everyone to lose but me, but I legitimately want to win every opportunity in my space and swim in a "blue ocean" of no competition. It's taken me years to be able to step outside of the emotion and subjectivity of an opportunity and recognize where that gut-wrenching anxiety comes from. In my opinion, it's a scarcity mindset that clouds my objective thoughts. It's that slight fear that this might be the last opportunity on earth, and my sales world is going to collapse if I don't win… just this one deal! I've had to retrain my brain to a abundance mindset and recognize the following:

   a. We've designed and executed a process. We must believe in the process, and adhere to the process. Deviating from that process by holding onto accounts and opportunities for emotional reasons is counter-intuitive and does a disservice to the process.
   b. There will always be another opportunity.

This all boils down to not getting sidetracked by the shiny deals. If it falls outside your designed process, the opportunity must be addressed objectively: "if time is what I can control, and I have to be masterful with my time, how would a third-party time optimization coach treat this opportunity? Based on all the objective data, and caring very little for the subjective back-story of this account, what does the process tell us to do?"

At Sales for Life, here is what we look for:

a. Did we objectively engage this account using a complete Activation Cycle?
b. Once we've completed the Activation Cycle, did we activate key stakeholders into the account and create a Sales Qualified Lead (SQL)?
c. Is the account engagement process older than 90 days?

We have all the data we need to make an objective decision. In 2017, we averaged 94 days to activate and win an account, with a median of 82 days. While there were a few outlier opportunities that stretched our model, there needed to be further objective evidence made into a structured business case to continue working that opportunity. In our fiscal year 2018, we reduced our that activation-to-win down to 57 days, with a median of 30 days! This was made possible by focusing relentlessly on **qualifying fast with a focused framework**.

How to qualify fast with a focused framework

In the example above, if we allowed subjectivity to cloud our pipeline coverage, we would fall into the death spiral of an inflated sense of pipeline. The best-in-class sales organizations use their Activation Cycle as a qualifying OUT mechanism. They make it harder for companies to fit into their "sweet spot". Within 30, 60 or 90 days, they're able to segment the Total Addressable Market (TAM) of a sales professional's territory, and know which accounts they should focus on for the remaining three quarters. This is especially important if you sell high ACV (>$100,000 deals) and/or have sales cycles that are longer than six months. If you or your sales team get caught falling in love with accounts for eight months, only to discover that sales professionals on your team are executing "random acts of account engagement," or not adhering to a process, without really knowing their TAM, you're in serious trouble. Qualify fast, qualify out fast.

As Chet Holmes eloquently labelled it in his book *The Ultimate Sales Machine*, less than 10% of your TAM is open to buy, and only 3% is ready to purchase. Priority number one for any sales professional and leader of a sales team needs to be territory mapping for that 3% market. Unless you sell to one account, you must treat your market with an abundance mindset and disqualify accounts.

Process breeds clarity

Early in our fiscal year 2018, I was frustrated with our sales production. I had a call with Chad Nuss at InsideOut Sourcing, and I just vented. I explained our current sales plateau, hoping he could shed some wisdom from his experience.

His main insight was pure gold: "Have you done a W.I.L.L. analysis?"

W.I.L.L. stands for What Ideal Looks Like, based on your past and current customer data, and it helps you develop your leading, current and lagging indicators for the type of customers you really want to win. In fact, I had never done this, so Chad gave me a template where we placed 25 data points into a spreadsheet, with picklist dropdown (so the data could be placed in pivot tables), and segmented the data into six categories:

1. **Demographics:** location, industry, size, revenue growth versus retraction
2. **Mindset before buying:** was the account focused on long-term behavioral change versus immediate sales results as a justification for social selling training?
3. **Content consumption/self-education before buying:** how prepared were key stakeholders to embark on a digital transformation?
4. **Customers self-procurement process versus the buying process we've designed for our customers:** did they follow our advice throughout the buying process, or stick to buying the way they've always bought sales training in the past?
5. **Implementation experience and engagement**: who was involved in leading the project, how engaged were they throughout the project, what learning behaviors and behavioral changes did the account have?

6. **Results, ROI, account stickiness**: Cost of Customer Acquisition vs. Lifetime Value, Average Contract Value, Expansion vs. "one and done"?

The results were bone-rattling: it was so obvious where we were making mistakes. Imagine giving your sales team the empirical evidence of exactly who they should focus their time on, otherwise risk a customer that churns and burns. Growing an organically scaled company like Sales for Life, it's REALLY hard to find your objectivity and turn down business (I'm particularly sensitive to remembering the days when our business was starting out and struggling to pay the bills), but the results and change in 90 days is undeniable! Once we focused on W.I.L.L. and sales bookings, gross margins and EBITA dramatically improved.

Question for you... have you created your W.I.L.L.?

Examples of what we learned:

a. **How fast does W.I.L.L. move from activated account (SAL)-to-customer?**
Remarkably fast. 50% of our engagements are decided in 30 days. While 45-90 days is average, crossing 90 days is a yellow flag. The data is obvious. If a champion can't pull together the buying committee and align their team on modernizing their pipeline creation process within one quarter, then digital selling de-prioritizes onto the "nice to have" list. After a activated account crosses 180 days, we have almost zero chance of putting together the project. 180 days is a huge red flag that something (a specific key stakeholder, priority shifts or budget) is not aligned to digital sales training.

b. **Is the existence of a sales enablement team, or their direct involvement, a leading indicator that skill-based learning is a priority?**
Hard yes! This is one of the first signs we look for in a company. While some enablement leaders view outsourced sales training as a threat to their own role, the top enablement teams realize they can't build, enable and scale a team on their own. There is a direct correlation between sales enablement

investment (resources and funding) and a customer's ability to drive a successful global project. Of course, SMB companies can be successful without sales enablement if sales leadership is committed to acting as a training resource and coach. What doesn't work, however, is a sales enablement leader that is treated like a second-class citizen in their sales organization, and can't gain the attention of sales leaders. Any sales enablement leader we've met that's trying to put digital sales training on their backs as a "career booster" is unfortunately too self-serving, and rarely gains the prioritization needed from sales leadership. If you're a sales enablement leader feeling like you live on an island, you have to gain sales leadership's full support first, otherwise you're doomed to fail.

c. **How critical is sales leadership involvement?**
Sales leadership involvement **is the difference** between success and failure. It's so important that this is where W.I.L.L. now starts and stops for Sales for Life. Without sales leadership support, we have to take a hard look at pausing or stopping our relationship. Trust me, it's just as hard on us as an organically funded company. But the data is so black and white: 100% of projects that didn't have sales leadership involved in the purchasing process, or heavily involved during the project implementation, have ALL become "one and done" projects. 100%! There is no sales enablement or marketing team EVER (and we've trained more than 300 companies around the world) strong enough to attempt a digital sales transformation without the involvement of sales leadership. 60% of the projects that lack sales leadership in just **the purchasing process** got delayed or cancelled.

The reason I share all these data points about Sales for Life is to help you reflect on evaluating your accounts that fall outside your objective process. Have we won outlier accounts before? Of course. Have they been successful? Most of the time... NO. Your designed process will continue to refine itself into green, yellow and red flags. When key stakeholders in an account are not adhering to your process that's designed to be customer-centric and learning-centric, you might be spending your time with the wrong account.

Chapter 22: Run - digitally surround your strengthened buying committee map

"There are no traffic jams along the extra mile."
– Roger Staubach

In August 2011, at my small consulting company Shanks Group (before its merger with Sales for Life), I leveraged the power of a social engagement to accelerate my opportunity in one account. I was on LinkedIn reviewing Profile Updates when a past business acquaintance, Terry Foster, changed his profile status to "Current Title: President, Cision Canada". As any good sales professional should, I used this opportunity to congratulate Terry on his new role. I clicked "Like" and commented: "Congratulations on your new role – as you grow your new sales team, don't hesitate to reach out." Terry sent me a LinkedIn message 24 hours after my comment, saying: "We should get together to discuss my new sales team." Within a week, I was in his office talking about a small consulting project that grew into an engagement that ran for two and a half years. Even seemingly small gestures like this can have a profound impact in an account. This was a simple gesture that changed my business (as Terry Foster is now on the board of advisors at Sales for Life).

In deciding to run with an account or group of accounts, your responsibility shifts from qualification to "doubling down", and digitally surrounding your buying committee. Your mission is to activate each of the key stakeholders (whether that's five people or fifteen) and ensure you:

a. Be organized to identify multiple relationship entry-points
b. Increase your relationship and exposure footprint
c. Never miss an opportunity to start a compelling conversation

Step 1: Strengthen your known buying committee map

Where you gather the data is less important than the data itself. You're responsible for knowing the hierarchy and connective relationships with your accounts. Our customers use various data sources, as no one source is perfect. LinkedIn is obviously fantastic, but if the key stakeholder hasn't updated their LinkedIn profile, or has a unique title that LinkedIn's AI can't correlate to specific role/function, your map will appear incomplete. Here are three tips that sales professionals have used to better equip themselves with stronger roadmaps:

A: Deploy a highly viral LinkedIn PointDrive

The best-in-class sales professionals realize that whichever digital tool will leave the best fingerprints around an account's "hallways" is the digital tool of choice. You will create LinkedIn PointDrives that are explicitly used as tracking devices. The insights within the PointDrive need to be valuable, unique, and interesting enough for key stakeholders to show their team in conference calls/boardrooms. These PointDrives are not an afterthought added at the bottom of your follow-up email, but treated like you're handing out vaccinations to a room of people with the flu. "Pass the flu shot around, and make sure everyone gets their medicine." There is no digital sales tool we've found more effective for buyer committee mapping than LinkedIn PointDrive. I can't tell you how many sales professionals have said weeks after leveraging this tool: "I found out that this CXO was part of the buying committee because she realized this project would affect her division. I had absolutely no idea she was involved, and if I didn't know she was looking at our project, I wouldn't have concentrated on working with her."

B: The prepared sales professional (proper business acumen questions)

At Sales for Life, team member Brian Lipp does this masterfully. Rather than asking your champion on a call "soooo, do you make the decisions? Do you have a budget?", Brian will do the following:

- Leverage tools like LinkedIn to visually build an organizational chart of the champions, potential decision-makers, and potential cross-functional influencers;
- Document these names and functions before the call/live meeting;
- Ask the champions the following question towards the end of the call: "I noticed Kathy runs Marketing and Kurt is in charge of Demand Generation, but they weren't on this call. How will this (our solution) impact their business?"

Brian is looking out for a few things:

- Champions that seem to want to go rogue without inviting others. Stating "this is my decision" is a big red flag. The decision is almost rarely theirs to make on their own.
- Champions that intimately understand their internal buying dynamics. If they know who is involved and how, then this might not be their first rodeo. If they appear uncertain, then we might have a champion that could get lost in the buying process.

We have never encountered a buyer that was frustrated by stopping to help properly roadmap the buying committee when it's framed from the lens of "success". Frankly, they're typically impressed with Brian's level of preparation.

C: The prepared sales professional (proper profiling for yellow/red flags)

When I'm about to walk into a meeting (whether that's in a live boardroom or on a conference call), I need to know the people I'm meeting and the situation I'm walking into. It's critical that I don't just profile those IN the boardroom or conference call. They are typically only a portion of the buying committee. My main scouting report is about risk mitigation and time management, as I've committed to RUN with this account. Was this a good choice?

Here are two critical elements on a LinkedIn profile (outside of shared connections in common) that I look for:

1. **Left Brain vs. Right Brain:** This is my assessment of a strategic vs. operational thinker, or what Gary Vaynerchuk would call "clouds and dirt". Typically there are two distinctive types of buyers (there are rare cases where key stakeholders share both brain types):
   a. **Right Brain** – typically associated with visualization, imagination and big thinking. These are the types of buyers that want to talk value drivers, not widgets and bo-bobs. Stick to aligning all your messages to saving money, making money or mitigating risk. I'm looking for the words people use in their profile to describe themselves: are they talking about big initiatives and the outcomes of those projects?
   b. **Left Brain** – typically associated with math, logic and sequence. These are the types of buyers that want to see your process and deliverables. They want the software demo. If they don't see HOW it works, the entire pitch falls apart. Look for people who talk about very detailed certifications, skills, projects on their profile that show a "work IN, not ON" mentality.

2. **Tenure (Do they know HOW to buy?)** I use a simple proxy of six months for myself. This is the timeline where my "spidey senses" start to tingle if a key stakeholder is newer than six months at the company. We all know that titles like CXO or VP of XYZ are important decision-making titles. And these buyers may go down a path with you with the full expectation that they WANT to buy. But do they know HOW to buy? People who are new to an organization (the larger the company, the more my red flags go up) are full of zest and energy to make the change. Unfortunately, they lack the internal experience to understand:

- When and how often are budgets released? Can budget be pulled cross-functionally?
- How did the company perform in the two quarters before your key stakeholder arrived, and what did the CFO say about spending on the all-hands meeting before they arrived?
- Do they have a policy that an overspend in a previous quarter results in a budget cut in future quarters?
- Does the company have a legal policy never to lock itself into SaaS agreements? Or long-term contracts?
- Historically, do they only buy in pilots?
- What is the vendor process? Do you need to be an approved vendor in a procurement process for PO number to be issued? Who has the authority to issue PO numbers?

There are SO many questions that I could continue with, and your key stakeholder will most likely NOT know the answer to these questions. Yes, they WANT to buy, but they don't know HOW to buy – and you're going to be the guinea pig!

Step 2: Leverage your four "lightbulbs" of social insights to focus

Buying intent triggers are available to you, so use them! Within LinkedIn and Vidyard GoVideo (two major tools for account-based selling), there are four "lightbulbs" that best-in-class sales professionals review every day. No exceptions. These triggers will help you sort accounts by buying intent, and help deepen your buyer committee map:

a. **LinkedIn "Who viewed your profile":** I personally review each profile and attempt to correlate why they've viewed my profile against accounts we're seeking to activate/have activated. Without fail, 24 hours before a major change in an account happens (such as they reach out again or set up a new meeting with us), the key stakeholders always seem to take a look at my LinkedIn profile.

b. **LinkedIn Notifications:** News, 1st-degree job changes, content comments, etc. can be an excellent leading indicator to sourcing account opportunities.

c. **LinkedIn PointDrive "Insights":** This is one of the most direct indicators of buying intent that we've seen, and one of the strongest buying committee mapping tools available.

d. **Vidyard GoVideo "Notifications":** Through 2019/2020, video will continue to be a key competitive differentiator for sales professionals. Buyers that watch your videos are demonstrating a key willingness to learn, which is often a leading indicator to buying intent. As with LinkedIn PointDrives, encourage your key stakeholders to share these videos amongst their team to help make the videos go viral. This only helps you further with buyer committee mapping.

Step 3: Super-size your engagement power with social comments

Back to my story about Terry Foster earlier in this chapter, where a simple gesture landed me a two-and-a-half-year contract (LTV of >$100,000 account), a new business advisor, and a new friend. This is where average sales professionals are surpassed by their best-in-class counterparts. The average sales professionals hit the "easy button". The easy button means clicking "Like" on key stakeholders' content on social media platforms like LinkedIn, Twitter, Facebook, etc. This "Like" is one amongst a plethora of other likes – with almost no exposure. The best-in-class sales professionals realize that to be top-of-mind, you have to act top-of-mind. These sales professionals will do the following:

    a. Using LinkedIn Sales Navigator, they will identify an account, and use the Lead Results tab to sort through all employees that "Posted on LinkedIn in the last 30 days";
    b. Sort through these employees and focus on potential key stakeholders;
    c. Read the content they've shared over the last 30 days;
    d. Comment and ADD VALUE to these articles, blogs, re-shares, etc. Don't comment if value can't be added, but comment if you can inspire further conversation. This creates an exposure footprint.

The results from a key stakeholder's perspective is pronounced. They'll receive a trifecta of notifications: via email, LinkedIn Notification, and, for many mobile users, "ping" notification on their mobile phone. While your competition most likely remains incognito to that key stakeholder, you're front and center. I can personally tell you that this method of engagement has allowed me to learn more about new products/services for my company, and we have absolutely purchased from these great sales tactics (Brandon Bornancin, CEO at Seamless.ai, is someone that's particularly great at this focused approach).

Chapter 23: REPLACE accounts with objectivity inside your account operating framework

"Every new beginning comes from some other beginning's end."
Seneca

If you have the autonomy to select, run or replace accounts in your territory, I'll pause and let you "set sail" one of your dormant/non-activated accounts…

Good. I know that was painful, but that's sales. Think of that loss as a "not now," rather than a "not at all."

Your objective is to build and adhere to a structured process, so let's outline a replacement strategy for your dormant/non-activated accounts. Objective sales professionals don't need to give their sales leaders a long back story as to why they're replacing an account – it should simply have failed your Activation Cycle litmus test.

Step 1: Bucket and tag the dormant/non-activated

Best-in-class sales organizations are meticulous about cataloging accounts. As the Chief Revenue Officer, it's imperative that you understand the TAM (Total Addressable Market) within each sales professional's territory, and the units and percentage of accounts that are categorized customers vs. prospective customers. This helps you determine the following:

> a. If we see a collectively large dataset of accounts not activating in EACH of my sales professionals' territories, is there a common theme (specific

verticals, size of accounts)? Should we be adjusting our engagement strategy?

b. If we see a collectively large dataset of accounts non-activating in specific sales professionals' territories, are we certain their following the process? Is there a particular skill/capability that they're lacking that has their metrics lagging from their peers?

You want to collect data on this activation process in the same manner you're most likely collecting opportunities-to-win ratios. How similar or dissimilar to the Chet Holmes pyramid (in which 3% of a market is actively purchasing) did your sales team indicate? This allows you to set quarterly and/or annual goals to find other ways to activate these accounts, and not use expensive sales resources. One common solution that our customers have been embracing more is working in closer collaboration with marketing on an ABM (account-based marketing) strategy. These marketing teams invest in tools like Engagio or Terminus to power their ABM learning paths. In this way, you've taken the workload out of the sales professionals' hands, and will attempt to activate these accounts with a more scalable/cost-effective resource.

Step 2: Develop a cadence timeline for "replacement dates"

Time management is in your control. Avoid allowing yourself or your sales team to replace a handful of accounts each time they've run through their Activation Cycle and failed to activate. I want you to think about the hundred or so pages you've just read, and think about the mental pivots you would have to make if you were selecting, planning/storyboarding and running competitive intelligence, all on new accounts, just on a random Wednesday morning. Intermix this with also trying to have three discovery calls and two proposal calls that day. This is time batching 101. Design your replacement cadence to coincide with a few variables:

a. When is the natural conclusion of an Activation Cycle, and how long does an account stay non-activated/dormant before stretching to average norms?

b. Do you have natural slow periods at certain times of each month or quarter that can allow you or your sales team some time to take one step back and plan?

As previously mentioned, at Sales for Life our timelines coincide nicely with our Quarterly Business Reviews (QBR). This is a perfect time for our team to review which accounts are going back into the marketing system, replace these accounts with new accounts (based on the Sphere of Influence) and recalibrate our engagement strategies for the next quarter.

Step 3: Diligence and accountability to your Activation Cycle – don't cheat yourself

Find an accountability "backstop" for yourself, such as an objective peer. If you're a sales leader, you're cheating the sales organization of opportunity cost if you neglect to adhere to your REPLACE operating framework. I want to leave you with this sobering math:

Each quarter, you subjectively allow a sales professional to hold onto one account beyond your recommended Activation Cycle (because they really trust the key stakeholders at the company, brand recognition, fear of looking your CEO in the eyes to tell her that we're not chasing that account, whatever the excuse…). You allow the sales professional to nurture that account, rather than select one new account each quarter that has very high social proximity, and might be a better fit for your business. This cycle repeats itself each quarter for the year. Those four "opportunity costed" accounts you didn't pursue, at a 25%-win conversion, could have accounted for one new customer each year. Your sales professional has a $1,000,000 sales quota, and the ACV (Average Contract Value) of that missed account would have been $100,000. Unfortunately, the sales professional falls short of your quota (like the other 50% of sales professionals, according a 2017 CSO Insights report). You have 100 sales professionals on your team, and you've allowed this subjective leniency for each of the 100 sales professionals. If you're not adhering to your own operating framework, that could mean the following scale issue:

- 4 "missed accounts" per quarter x 100 sales professionals = 400 accounts in Total Addressable Markets (TAM) that were non-activated due to "opportunity cost". Try to explain to a Board of Directors why you've fallen short of your market share penetration goals.

- 1 "new deal" at \$100,000 ACV x 100 sales professionals = \$10,000,000 you didn't find and win. This could be equivalent to your company's entire sales bookings growth goal for the year. If your ACV is \$100,000, let's not even imagine what the "opportunity cost" of the LTV (Lifetime Value) of those accounts could have been. Explain that one to the CFO.

I recognize my example is extreme, but you can't easily see the ill-effects that holding onto accounts too long can have on an organization. Be diligent in adhering to your operating framework, and find accountability backstops if necessary.

Conclusion

Fishing with the proverbial *spear* (account-based) is unquestionably a more difficult sales motion than a *net* (open account) focus. Many open account sales professionals will field inbound inquiries as part of their lead source mix, and nothing makes a sales professional smile like an inbound lead. When I wrote *Social Selling Mastery*® in 2016, the focus of social selling at that time was centered around being both a magnet for inbound leads and opportunistic in your outbound prospecting. For growing sales organizations, being a magnet in a territory is not enough to reach sales quota attainment. Sales professionals have to complement this motion with account-based focus, whether outbound prospecting for new accounts, or up-selling/cross-selling the existing account base.

Most growth companies find inbound lead flow not nourishing enough, as they don't get to choose the fish that land in their inbound net. High growth sales organizations require higher ACV (Average Contract Value) per account to reach their accelerated Compounded Annual Growth Rate (CAGR) targets.

These important "tunas, marlins and whales" are found in the deep water, making them harder to obtain. Sales for Life developed its account-based sales training curriculum out of a desire to transform sales organizations into modern, digital machines that can exceed these high growth targets.

I know from watching social selling evolve between 2011 and 2018 that a digital account-based sales approach will "half-life" its adoption in sales organizations. I envision that digital account-based sales will transition from a motion that only best-in-class "early adopters" leverage to become standard operating procedure for thousands of companies within five years. Already nipping at the heels of high social proximity account selection is/will be the complement of propensity scoring, using artificial intelligence and machine learning.

Ultra-elite sales organizations have already begun refining their account selection (outbound) and inbound leads based on a combination of social proximity and propensity scoring. This leads to conversion rates soaring, and far better time management for sales professionals.

I consider this book to be the beginning of a new age of digital account-based selling, with incredible advances to come over the next five to ten years. I look forward to continuing the sales journey with you!

Made in the USA
Columbia, SC
17 February 2019